C'MON, MAN!

C'MON, MAN!

Taking on the Challenges Faced by Men

CHRIS ROBINSON

Clovercroft Publishing

C'mon, Man!

©2021 by Chris Robinson

Published by Clovercroft Publishing, Franklin, TN.

Published in association with Larry Carpenter of Christian Book Services, LLC.
Franklin, TN.

Edited by Ann Tatlock

Cover and Interior Design by Suzanne Lawing

Printed in the United States of America

ISBN: 978-1-950892-87-7

Contents

FOREWORD

This book is written for you, no matter your age or stage in life. It represents areas of learning we will all need at one point or another and lessons we will want to pass along to those who follow us. It's written to help you learn more about yourself, the struggles you might deal with and ways in which you can move forward with renewed confidence in who you are and who you can be. It can be read individually or in a group setting. Although a flow is created in the order of the chapters, it doesn't have to be read in any particular order to be useful. There may be chapters that resonate with you and others you feel are of no benefit. That's okay. We're all created uniquely with our own sets of skills and competencies and our own areas of struggle. This book isn't intended to put you in the same box with every other man. Read what is helpful. It is also written for those who love you. Share it with them. Discuss it with them. Give yourself permission to be vulnerable with them. I had to do this in the writing – you should do so in the reading.

This book could only have been written because of those who love me, have lived with me, and have taught me. Chief among them are my wife, Denise, and my two daughters, Stephanie and Alyssa. They are my world. I thank the friends who know me and still choose to make me part of their lives – particularly David Taylor and Sonny Gann. I thank the numerous groups I'm a part of for sharing words of wisdom with me. There are so many people who have spoken truth into my life I cannot possibly mention them all, but each and every one of them has planted a seed that has taken root and bloomed. Thank you all.

Chris Robinson, 2021

INTRODUCTION

We've all seen the videos ... those moments in sports where professional athletes have an absolute brain lapse in performing what should be the basic skills of their trade. Missing a tackle, dropping a pass, running the wrong way, missing a layup, making a bad play worse ... all of which are followed by those dreaded words from the announcer ... "C'MON, MAN!" They are hilarious, surprising, unbelievable and, unfortunately for the athlete, unforgettable. While the rest of us entertain ourselves with the video replays of the gaff, the athlete is sitting in a film room somewhere with a coach who is also replaying it over ... and over ... and over again. Again ... and again ... and again, making the athlete witness his own error as a learning tool, as though it was not indelibly and perpetually seared into his memory from the moment it happened. You can almost FEEL the pain! We wouldn't wish that moment on our worst enemy ... but we still get a laugh out of it.

As much as we hate to admit it, we all have our "C'mon, man" moments. We're just fortunate they don't get recorded and replayed in front of the whole world - that is, unless somebody captures it on their phone and turns us into an unwilling YouTube celebrity. These moments might occur in the form of a physical or a mental blunder. They might occur in our community, in our workplace, or in our living room – but they occur and they are embarrassing.

The statement "C'mon, man" reflects complete disbelief. It's exasperation. It's frustration. It's disappointment. It's criticism coming from outside and coming from within. It's the phrase we subconsciously play in our head when we feel we have failed to measure up to expectations. "C'mon, man" is about not getting it right. Sometimes it's about externalizing our own frustrations with others when, despite our best efforts, we're criticized – when we want to cry out "C'mon, man! What do you want from me? Give me a break!"

We live in a fast-paced world where the expectations are high and growing higher every day. From the day we were born we've been reinforced based on performance. A little boy playing with dolls is met with discouragement … "C'mon, man." Throwing a ball is met with encouragement … "Attaboy!" Sensitivity to being called names in elementary or middle school is met with a chiding to toughen up … "C'mon, man." Fighting back is rewarded … "Way to go!" Young men who don't display enough competitive fire are labeled as under-achievers … "C'mon, man." Those who do whatever it takes to win are promoted … "You're a born leader!" Men who cry are said to lack internal strength … "C'mon, man." Those who are stoic are admired … "The guy is a rock!" In this "C'mon, man" world, it's no wonder many men struggle silently with issues leading to problems with self-image, anxiety, and depression.

We struggle to get it right and feel the daily pressure of failing in some aspect of our performance as a son, a sibling, a husband, or a father. We question our direction and our effectiveness as leaders. We wonder if we're respected. We doubt our effectiveness in dealing with transitions that sometimes leave us feeling unprepared and off balance. We build resentment and mistrust in the actions of others as we grasp for control over things outside of our control. All these things can leave us operating out of fear and feeling isolated, questioning our own worth as men. If you've found yourself identifying with any of this, keep on reading – because this isn't how we're meant to live.

We are not meant to live lives in which we're simply reacting to whatever external criteria are affecting us. We are not meant to be blown aimlessly off course by overpowering winds. We are meant to harness the wind for an exhilarating ride, not to be taken for a ride that scares us. Let me say to you right here and right now: you have complete control over your ride. But to harness control involves developing certain skill sets, purging false beliefs about who you are and overcoming fears that hold you back. You and you alone have the ability to control the way you think and the choices you make. Up to this point, the narrative of your life may have been written based on what others have said *about* you or to you. That does not make it true of you.

If you've grown tired of the pressure and disappointments of the "C'mon, man" world we live in, I invite you to move beyond the deafening criticisms of unmet expectations that may have been launched at you or that you've made of yourself. Let's examine the issues limiting your ability to enjoy life and learn how to gain and exercise control over them. Let me encourage you to look at who you are in a new light. Let me help you explore your true self and the untapped strength you have for not only controlling but for redirecting your life. Let me reframe that antagonistic "C'mon, man" to an enthusiastic invitation for you to join me in discovering how you can experience higher quality of life and be the man you are created to be … "C'mon, man."

I

EXPLORING VALUES

I spent thirty-five years in the construction industry and built projects throughout the Southeast and the Southwest. This resulted in many moves for me and my family. One of those moves was made from Dyersburg, Tennessee to Dallas, Texas in 1998. If you're old enough, you'll remember this was the time of the Beanie Baby craze. Beanie Babies were little bean bag animals. I can't say how many different types of Beanie Babies there were, but it seems like thousands! They were a stroke of marketing genius – they were simple, easy to make, and there was not a child known to exist on the planet who could survive without several of them. My daughters, nine and eleven at the time, were no exception.

My younger daughter, Alyssa, who had amassed around a hundred Beanie Babies, was particularly concerned about the safety of them during this move. She was concerned they would somehow be lost or stolen and asked if we could bring them to Texas ourselves rather than having them packed with the household goods. As is the case with most business-related moves, I was required to relocate to my new assignment in Texas ahead of my family since our girls were still in school in Tennessee. I was going to drive our Suburban with the limited belongings I needed for the apartment I had leased for a few months in Dallas. This became the perfect opportunity to provide safe passage for Alyssa's Beanie Babies to their new home in Texas, which I did successfully. Mission accomplished.

At the end of the school year, we timed our "full family" move strategically. I would vacate my apartment in Dallas, fly back to Tennessee, return to Texas in our minivan with my wife, daughters and dog, and move directly into our new home. Everything went off without a hitch and we spent the weekend getting our things moved in. On Monday morning, my wife drove me to the airport to retrieve the Suburban containing my belongings. I drove to the office in my car and she returned home to spend the day unpacking. Neither of us encountered a problem. Mission accomplished.

That day, as I left the office for lunch, I noticed something strange about the back of my car. As I approached it, I saw what I hadn't seen when retrieving the car at the airport - someone had used a screwdriver on the rear door lock to break into it. I felt my heart race from fear that everything had been stolen. I quickly opened the back door and felt both relief and disbelief to find everything in its place - until I took a second glance. There was only one thing taken – Alyssa's bag full of Beanie Babies. If you're a father, you will understand my devastation in that moment.

As fathers, one of our jobs is, to the best of our ability, protecting our children from bad things. I took on this responsibility in offering to protect my daughter's most prized possessions and she entrusted me to do so. I had failed her. I called my wife to let her know what happened and asked her to let me tell Alyssa when I got home that evening. I dreaded seeing the look in her eyes when I gave her the news and could not think of words to express how deeply I regretted letting her down. It was a long afternoon.

When I got home, I received my daughters' excited updates on their first day of swim team practice, the new friends they had made and the plans they already had for the rest of the week. My joy in their excitement was overshadowed by what I now had to tell Alyssa. I sat down to be at her eye level and she asked me about her Beanie Babies.

I gently explained to her the car had been broken into and her Beanie Babies had been stolen. As I watched her eyes turn down, I told her how sorry I was for disappointing her and that I knew how much they meant to her. I tried to find words to express my regret and ask her forgiveness. As I silently searched for the right thing to say to soothe her, she re-established eye contact with me and said "Don't worry, Dad. It's only stuff"… and she meant it. I could see she made an on-the-spot self-examination of what was important to her, and it was not Beanie Babies.

At that moment, my nine-year-old daughter taught me about values.

A soul-searching exploration of values has to be the start of any man's journey. From the day of our birth our core values are shaped as we form relationships, gather information and experience life. Through childhood, adolescence, and early adulthood these values continuously evolve and solidify. As we mature into young adulthood, our mid-twenties to early thirties, they become well established. These are deeply rooted values and create a sense of self-identity.

When I was in my fifties, my career focus changed and I decided to make a radical transition. To be more engaged in helping people, I chose to leave the field of construction for the profession of counseling. One of my areas of focus is helping men work through common struggles, which each man generally believes is unique to him. In truth, most of us deal with the same issues. When I work with men who are trying to establish their direction or figure out where they got off track, I start with values. On the next page, "Table A" has a list of values for you to consider. It's important to recognize, within this list, there are no right or wrong values. Values are passed down, learned, and developed based on each person's experiences. Values differ from society to society, culture to culture, ethnicity to ethnicity and nation to nation. What's important is for you to know your own values. Take a moment now to do this by looking at the list of words in the Values List on the next page. Add to them if you don't see values important to you, and see if you can choose and rank the top five values in your life.

VALUES LIST

Success	Image	Security	Wealth
Justice	Vocation	Equality	Acceptance
Self-identity	Education	Solitude	Independence
Integrity	Honesty	Teamwork	Freedom
Stability	Comfort	Self-esteem	Power
Money	Faith	Health	Home
Possessions/Property	Recreation	Control	Sexuality
Nature/Environment	Family	Excitement	Poverty
Relationship	Friendship	Appearance	Community
Quality	Individuality	Harmony	Perfection
Openness	Privacy	Forgiveness	Spirituality
Religion	Joy	Recognition	Companionship
Peace	Safety	Diversity	Adventure
Travel	Love	Helping	Respect
Creativity	Wisdom	Variety	Unity
Competition	Patriotism	Winning	Popularity
Affirmation	Career	Order	Advancement
Connection	Growth	Status	Accomplishment
Purpose	Time	Autonomy	Validation

If you've never given thought to your core values before, this exercise may have been difficult. You may have become stuck with the meaning of the words. Don't worry about it. Words can have different meanings to different people because their meaning is directly correlated to each individual's life experiences. You can provide your own meaning to the words based upon your life experiences and understanding. Remember – your core values are based on what is important to you, and not on anyone else's expectations or externally influenced beliefs about what should be important. For instance, you might think no one would have a core value of poverty. But reconsider this from the perspective of someone who has taken a vow of poverty. Whatever values you selected, be okay with the truth of those values in your life but don't allow yourself to be fooled. If you find yourself feeling continuously restless or bored with the choices you've made for your life, check your values. Either those choices may not reflect your true core values or they aren't properly prioritized.

Maybe identifying your core values was easy, but ranking them was more difficult. This is where being honest with yourself becomes critical if you're going to have peace of mind in the way you live and order your life. It requires identification of, above all other things, the most important thing to your existence. This means you would forfeit all else to assure this one core value was being fulfilled in your life. Likewise, as you continue to prioritize, your second core value would reflect the next most important thing in your life, for which you would be willing to forfeit all else besides your first core value. And so on. The tough part of this is you can't ride the fence. You must decide the rank order. There are no ties. This is important because you never know when there will be a crossroad in your life requiring a decision to be made. Take, for example, a man who values work and family equally because he finds his identity in both. His job is demanding, so he sacrifices time with family. He believes that in fulfilling his work responsibilities he also fulfills his family responsibilities. This goes on for years. He is stunned when he comes home one day to find his wife has filed for divorce. He has met his crossroad but blew through it at eighty miles an hour and had a serious wreck. He didn't see it coming because he was unaware that his behavior – placing work ahead of family – was inconsistent with his claim that the two were equally valued.

By prioritizing core values you're establishing a mindset. You're literally making up your mind regarding what is most important in life, which generally determines your actions and behaviors. Your behaviors should be reflective of what is truly most important to you. When honest about prioritizing core values, you're better able to make decisions before reaching a crossroad. You set boundaries around the most important values, establishing limits or lines which will not be crossed. These boundaries might be related to your office hours, the number of evenings you entertain clients, checking work emails while at home, or any other number of work habits developed, perhaps, in contradiction to your core values.

Jim, a past associate of mine, established a boundary which demonstrated true commitment to his core value of family. He worked in an environment where long hours were the norm and were expected. He also had children whose events generally occurred late in the afternoon or early in the evening. He was committed as a father to being present for these events, so he decided to start his day at 5:00 a.m. instead of 7:00 a.m. This allowed him to leave the office as necessary not only to attend his children's events, but in the case of his son's sports, to help out as a coach. He conditioned his staff to come to him for any needed support prior to his time of departure. This not only created an efficient and productive office environment but affirmed commitment to his core value of family. In doing so, he earned a high level of respect both at work and at home.

You may have concerns over the flexibility your job will allow you. If this is the case, be aware you're approaching a crossroad. Slow down and evaluate the decisions to be made and the actions to be taken in order to safely navigate the intersection and continue on your intended path. Explore and discuss all viable options with others who are affected by your decision. Then, make the decision based upon your prioritized core values and take the action to place protective boundaries around them. Whatever you do, stay the course fulfilling the commitment to your own core values.

Beliefs

It's easy to confuse values with beliefs, but they are distinct and different. It's important to discuss this difference. Otherwise, we may be conflicted when we reasonably change our mind related to certain issues. We've already defined values as being developed through relationships, information, and experiences and as being fairly well established by young adulthood. There is less of a tendency for values to change given the time over which they are developed. Beliefs are built on the foundation of our values and are also established by relationships, information, and experiences. Beliefs, unlike values, are more apt to change. However, this doesn't mean our values have been compromised. In the world of politics when someone changes their mind, they are considered indecisive and weak on issues – "flip-floppers" or "sell-outs." I would argue that someone who formulates beliefs on sound logic and reasoning, yet is willing to change those beliefs in light of new relationships, information, or experiences, is demonstrating wisdom.

Let's use the story of Alyssa's Beanie Babies as an example of how beliefs can change without compromising values. Her Beanie Babies were of high importance to her. She had an attachment to them because she played with them and imagined them as living beings requiring care. This is a natural and important part of childhood development. Children, from infancy, learn about healthy attachment from their caregivers. They inherently understand and observe the nurturing they receive and transfer this nurturing in their style of play. As children grow older, they learn more about relationships and bonding through play with other children and with dolls – like Beanie Babies – and new attachments are created. Playing is one of the methods by which children come to understand and rehearse relationships. By nine years old, Alyssa had already established relationships as a core value. She had an attachment not only to me, but to the Beanie Babies she was afraid of losing. When she saw my disappointment in letting her down, she took only moments to realize her relationship to me was much more important than her relationship to the Beanie Babies – even changing her reference to the Beanie Babies as "only stuff." Her core value of having relationships didn't change, but her belief about those relationships did.

Core values are less likely to change than beliefs. Change in beliefs will generally occur with the introduction of new relationships, new information, and new experiences. Our beliefs are based upon understanding of the knowledge we possess. If knowledge is lacking, it stands to reason that understanding is also lacking. As we gain knowledge through new relationships, information and experience, we have the opportunity to increase our understanding. With increased understanding we are able to discern whether or not our previously held beliefs are still reasonable and then exercise wisdom in either maintaining or changing those beliefs.

The problem is, in many cases, change is not endorsed. Others are not as excited about it as we are. In fact, they are often skeptical as to the reasons for it and personalize your decision as a reflection of your relationship with them, which it may or may not be. If they're people you've been around for a very long time it's probably because you've always been like-minded and they want to keep it that way. When you move away from their way of thinking or doing, it can create an uncomfortable gap. The apple cart has been rocked and they don't understand why. We see this when someone changes their party affiliation in politics, when someone changes their church affiliation, when someone leaves their job, and even when someone leaves their marriage or partnership. Changing beliefs, or even values, may be the best thing you ever do, but don't do it on a whim. Because just as there are wise decisions, there are foolish decisions. Well-grounded values and beliefs will lead to a higher level of consistency in life and a greater feeling of fulfillment. Loosely grounded values and beliefs will increase chaos in your life and leave you feeling empty. When you have enough information to affirm your true values and beliefs, make your decision to either change course or stay the course and do so with confidence. Once you do, you can begin to experience more enjoyment in your quality of life and experience better life balance.

Summary Points of EXPLORING VALUES

- Values develop as we mature.

- Values reinforce a sense of self-identity.

- Values differ from person to person and culture to culture.

- Values must be identified and explored.

- Values should be prioritized.

- Beliefs with our value systems evolve based on development of relationships, new information, and new experiences.

Questions for Reflection

- Does evaluating long-held beliefs and values affect your self-awareness in any way?

- What formerly held beliefs of yours have changed based upon development of relationships, learning new information, and having new experiences?

- What are your top three prioritized values and how will you change habitual behavioral, mental, or verbal patterns to reflect these values?

2

LIFE BALANCE

As I advanced in my construction career and had more people reporting to me, it wasn't unusual to occasionally receive the question: "How did you figure out your work/life balance?" To be honest, there may have been better people to ask, because I initially got it all wrong.

I met my wife, Denise, in our senior year of college. What I can tell you about Denise is she is beautiful both inside and out. She is loving, wise, and enjoyable to be around. Someone would have to be trying their absolute hardest not to like her. Needless to say, I fell for her completely. And as we say in the unruly group of guys I run with today, "Thank God for beautiful women with poor taste in men!" Of course, we say this in fun. Unfortunately, in my case, there is too much truth to it because, to be blunt, I was one selfish bastard. I was fun to be around - as long as I was having fun. That means if I didn't like what we were doing, I didn't do it. She on the other hand was very unselfish so, in my mind, we made the perfect pair. We were engaged our senior year and each decided to work for a year before marrying. She started a career in accounting in San Angelo, Texas and I started my construction career in Dallas. What I can tell you about these two cities is there is far more to do in Dallas than in San Angelo and I took full advantage of all Dallas had to offer. I was out nearly every night at some sporting event or happy hour with friends from work. The weekends I didn't go to San Angelo or Denise didn't come to Dallas would be one long party with the guys. This was my lifestyle for the year prior to our marriage.

We were married on June 25, 1983, and had a wonderful honeymoon in Kauai, Hawaii. Then the honeymoon literally ended, nearly taking our marriage with it. Denise had left her job to move to Dallas, knowing very few people there and looking forward to her life with me. I also looked forward to my life with her - and to my continued lifestyle with my friends. For the first year of our marriage, I didn't make her my priority. I was so selfish I couldn't see what this did to her. I would make plans without discussing them – I would just tell her. She would express her displeasure when I came home late after drinking or spent the weekend with friends. I considered her complaints to be selfish and unreasonable on her part. To me, her pleas for more of my time sounded like incessant nagging. She never raised her voice to me until one morning when she was so frustrated she had to ask: "Do you even want to be married?" My response was the three words I still most regret in our marriage: "I don't know." I still remember her running out of the room in tears.

One. Selfish. Bastard.

That was my soul-searching moment. That was when I had to look at the model of the loving relationship my parents had given me and the value I had always placed on family. That was when I had to recall the life lessons I had learned about working together and being a team. That was when I had to remember my experience of coming to faith. It was then I realized how far I had veered off-path. I had to make a course correction because I had lost the bearing on my values and allowed my life to fall completely out of balance. I consider myself fortunate to have learned from my mistakes and that my story has a happy ending, because too many do not. I'm glad to say Denise and I will soon celebrate forty years of marriage … and all except the first have been happy!

Through accumulated relationships, information, and experience, I gained understanding and wisdom allowing me to provide better counsel to those following behind me. Feeling more qualified at this point of my life to answer the question of work/life balance, my first response is to just call it life balance. The term work/life balance implies work and life are two separate compartments. Our tendency is to look at work/life balance as a pie chart having two halves. The idea of separating your work life from your family life makes sense. It isn't good to take your work home with you. It's easy to say "leave your job at the front door," but it's not easy to do. How can we put out of our head something already heard or done or said? I've always been amused when a courtroom judge advises a jury to disregard a remark. How?!?! We can't un-say what has been said, un-hear what has been heard, or un-do what has been done. So how can we leave our work at the door? Our life is not a pie chart; it is one big pie – the entirety of our existence. It involves our vocation, our friendships, our family, our household chores, our recreation, our faith, our finances, and much more ... all of which are interwoven. When we're enjoying a slice of life, we are tasting every ingredient. Everything happening to us in one area of our life has a spillover effect to another area of our life. A fight with a roommate before leaving for work can leave you in a bad mood for the rest of the day. A bad vacation experience can leave you resentful, irritable, and grouchy. On the other hand, the birth of a child can have you walking on air. Nobody could ruin your day, even if they tried, because their bad mojo just slides right off you. What happens in one area of your life and the way you choose to respond affects all areas of your life. You can choose your mood – nobody chooses it for you. You can choose how you view situations - nobody can choose your perspective for you. You can even choose where you spend your time – all day, every day. The choices you make will ultimately impact your satisfaction with life balance. This is why value-based decisions discussed in Chapter 1, EXPLORING VALUES, are so important.

Like it or not, we must work to survive. Since work is an undeniable part of life, let's look at the math related to our work life. In pursuit of our career and, ultimately, our retirement, many of us take the socially-imposed path that follows: Elementary School, Middle School, High School, College, Work, Retire when eligible for Social Security. For Social Security retirement benefits, assuming you were born in 1960 or later, the retirement age is currently sixty-seven. As of 2015, the average lifespan of men in the U.S. is seventy-nine years. Let's do the math:

Birth thru Pre-K:	6 years
Primary through Secondary School:	13 years
College (on average):	4 years
Work (more if college is skipped):	44 years
Retirement to Death (uplifting, I know):	12 years
Total	**79 years**

Average percentage of life men in the U.S. spend in the workforce: 44 years / 79 years = 55.7%

With such a great investment of time in our vocation it's going to have a large impact on life balance and, therefore, quality of life. This makes vocation a good place for any man to start evaluation of life balance, regardless of age. I say "regardless of age" because men, no matter how old, need to discover life balance and encourage boys, no matter how young, to do the same.

If you're a young man, it's never too early to start exploring what you're truly passionate about doing – as opposed to what someone else expects you to do. Follow your passion or area of enjoyment from the beginning and seek fulfillment of this passion. You don't want to find yourself tied to a vocation providing no personal pleasure, purpose, or meaning. If you're doing something you don't enjoy, change what you're doing.

If you are a father, a grandfather, or an adult mentor, you can start coaching and encouraging boys and young men to follow their own passion today. Don't give in to the temptation to equate their success with status, wealth, or possessions. Success should be measured by life balance and life satisfaction. It isn't the man who dies with the most toys who wins – he just dies.

If you're a man in the workforce and you are dissatisfied with your life balance and quality of life due to your job, don't quit your job. First evaluate your values, priorities, passion, and budget and, if you are able, then quit your job and start doing something to fulfill them. I left my thirty-five-year career in construction in my fifties to start a new career in counseling. I was passionate about counseling. It provided more meaning and purpose in my life. I recognize there is also a different reality for men who are rapidly approaching retirement and considering implications of 401K distributions, pensions, and social security benefits. To these men, if you're not fulfilled in your job and it's absolutely too late to change without considerable cost, honestly consider both the costs and benefits (personally and financially) of change and then make your decision. If the costs are too high, stay with it – you're only a few years away from the life balance and quality of life you've earned and have been waiting for!

If you're already in the workforce and find fulfillment, purpose, meaning, and passion in your vocation - congratulations! You may find you love your job so much you spend most of your time at the office or doing work from home. However, you may be in a position where you have to find balance between your personal enjoyment of work and spending time with your friends or loved ones apart from work. Remember the old saying: "All work and no play makes Jack a dull boy." Don't be dull. Be disciplined.

It takes discipline to create life balance. With many of my clients who find themselves in a rut, one of the first things I'll do is have them create an activity chart showing what they do every hour of every day (even sleep). This can be used in a couple of ways. First, you can use it to record what you're actually doing during every hour. We generally don't think about how efficient or inefficient we're being with our time, but there is only so much time in a day and we don't want to waste it. Did we spend three hours doing a one-hour job? Did we spend four hours in front of the television? Did we spend two hours on Facebook, Instagram, Snapchat, etc? When we document how we're actually spending our time, we become more disciplined about using it to achieve life balance based on our values. The other way this activity chart can be used is as a planner. What time will you wake up in the morning and what will you do? Shower, read the e-paper, have coffee, eat breakfast? Set your alarm to let you start the day the way you want it to start. If you usually leave the office anywhere between 5:00 and 6:30 in the evening, show a 5:00 departure on the planner and stick to it. This may require better time management during your work day, which has its own benefits in terms of feelings of accomplishment and productivity. When you set a time to leave, set the time for where you are going. Maybe it's out to dinner with friends or home to dinner with loved ones. Maybe it's to take a class you have been interested in but never found time for. What happens after that? Time alone for reading, gaming, watching television, etc? What time do you want to get to bed for a good night's sleep and be able to wake up at the designated time the next morning? You get the point – whatever is of value to you should have its time slot according to your priorities. Without this discipline, you'll end up where I was after my first year of marriage – aimlessly wandering farther and farther away from what was most important to me. Once you've been at it for a while you'll hit your life balance stride. This is when spending time on what you most value becomes second nature. Don't allow your time to be stolen from the people or things meaning the most to you. Seek what fulfills your passion and provides you with meaning and purpose and focus your time there. By doing so, you'll put yourself in the driver's seat and feel more in control of your life.

Summary Points of LIFE BALANCE

- Life balance requires prioritized values.

- Life is one big pie – it can't be compartmentalized into a subdivided pie chart.

- Every slice of the pie includes a taste of every area of life – all areas of life are interwoven.

- Choices we make impact our satisfaction with life balance.

- Choose your vocation carefully – you'll spend 55% of your entire lifespan in it.

- Create a daily activity chart to determine what you currently spend time doing.

- Create an activity chart reflecting the life balance you desire.

Questions for Reflection

- Are your prioritized values reflected in your life balance?

- Are there any societal, vocational, or organizational norms or expectations causing you to be dissatisfied with your life balance?

- What would you need to do "less of" if you were honest with yourself about aligning values with life balance?

3

CONTROL

The dream of every human being is to be free. But what does it mean to be free? There are far too many instances in history where freedom for certain groups or individuals was bought at the expense of the freedom of others. Freedom is not intended to provide any person or group a blank check for wielding power over others. Therefore, some degree of regulation is required in any free society if its citizens are to have quality of life. These regulations, when properly applied, should control the use of power for the protection of all. Just as the proper use of control is important in any society, it's also important for every individual. It allows us to enjoy personal freedom and be in right relationship with others. When we learn to exercise self-control, we find we are less likely to allow the troubles of this world to overpower us. In this chapter, when we use the word "control" it's important to understand that personal control is about regulating ourselves. When we learn to regulate ourselves, we are more likely to be free from issues such as overwhelming anxiety or crippling depression. We are able to learn how to control internalized thoughts and feelings, which correlate with how we treat ourselves. We are also able to learn control of externalized emotions which can have a direct impact on how we treat others.

How We Treat Ourselves

In 1971 I was eleven and my family had just moved from New Jersey to Texas. A few months after our move my oldest brother, who was fifteen, was killed in a car accident. This devastated all of us – me, my parents and my four surviving siblings. We couldn't even begin to process what had happened and the loss we experienced. Our world was shaken, and our family system was turned upside down in an instant. A deafening silence overcame us.

My parents grew up in a time when mental health was not discussed; therefore the thought that counseling might help their surviving children never entered their mind. This is not a criticism of my parents – seeking mental help was just not a way of life when I was growing up. We all processed our grief and pain in different ways and over different time periods. Many of our coping mechanisms, including mine, were unhealthy. I went through the grief process and came through the trauma by suppressing my pain. I can personally testify that suppressing pain isn't healthy and doesn't work. The pain doesn't go away – it hides. When I turned fourteen, I had more independence and more access to resources and friends. I found new ways to escape my pain and began self-medicating with alcohol and marijuana. In those days it was rare for liquor stores or bars to ask minors to show identification for age verification. As for marijuana, well, times haven't changed – it's available anywhere for the person who wants it. Because access was easy, I ended up drinking and smoking frequently. The bars of choice for me and my other teenage friends were the strip clubs and porn bars. I was drinking and smoking to numb the pain and watching movies of girls in exotic acts to stimulate feelings. I am fortunate my drinking and smoking didn't lead to alcoholism and drug addiction. I was one of the fortunate who was able to slow it down. This is probably because I played football and the pain of football practices after a weekend of drinking and smoking was not worth the indulgence. The pornography, however, rang the bells of every reward center in my brain and became a problem for me. I found I had no self-control when it came to porn. In fact, the porn had complete control over me - its talons firmly embedded. As an adult, I would spend hours in secretive viewing of porn. This would be followed by feelings of shame and guilt for having thrown away what would have been valuable time with my family. Instead, I found myself viewing material supporting the exploitation and sexual abuse of women, which only contributed to more guilt and shame. I was violating my own values on many levels. I was left empty and embarrassed with myself. Upon returning home and seeing my beautiful wife and daughters, the guilt and shame would increase more. But I would repeatedly do the same thing when I was alone because I couldn't control my impulse.

I knew how my choices and behavior were affecting me. I was conflicted in every way … as a spouse, as a father, and as a Christian. Yes – I was also actively involved in my church. Now before you label me a hypocrite, let me beat you to the punch. I am. I always have been. I always will be. It's the reason I need a church. Now I'll continue.

Because of my leadership in the church I was asked to sit on a committee formed to initiate a program for those with addictions. Ironic, yes? I am firmly convinced God has a sense of humor. Why? Well… the head of the committee, David, suggested toward the end of our initial meeting that every one of us deals with some type of addiction. It could be anything from watching television, to lying, to drugs, to alcoholism, to gambling, to shopping, or to anything else we really can't seem to control. He thought it would be good, if we were to be genuine in our endeavor, to each name our own struggle.

There is a neurobiological reaction within our brain when we find ourselves in fearful situations – not slightly fearful, but feeling truly threatened. A brain component called the amygdala, which houses our fear response, starts firing signals to the rest of our body, communicating danger. It's known as the "fight-or-flight mode." You're probably familiar with it. Your heart rate increases, you begin sweating, your muscles tense, and your focus becomes intensely narrow. I can't remember a time when my fight-or-flight mode fired stronger than at David's suggestion to reveal our addiction. I literally felt like a caged wild animal. I sat physically still and quiet in my chair as my brain reeled and my emotions went into overdrive. My mind was racing and my heart was pounding so hard I could hear it in my ears. When you are in fight-or-flight mode, your fear center takes over and your executive brain function – your ability to think clearly - shuts down. All I could think of was lying or leaving, and my brain was not functioning clearly enough to even come up with a lie. Leaving would be a clear "tell" of a serious problem I was running from. I truly felt like a trap had sprung on me. Luckily, the confessions didn't start with me and I had time to breathe deeply and calm myself, albeit only slightly, before my turn came around. When the dreaded moment came and David's eyes met mine, all I could say was, "I have a struggle I've never spoken of before. I can't talk about it here before I talk about it with my wife." David was gracious toward me because he had previously spoken openly of his own drug and alcohol addictions and the embarrassment they caused him. He looked into my eyes, knowingly, and simply said, "I understand." I went home that night and had the most difficult conversation I've ever had with my wife. She listened calmly and quietly as I laid out my confession and then she gave her response: "I love you. You are my knight in shining armor."

Need I say more about my beautiful Denise?

At the following meeting of the addiction group planning committee, I returned to the previous week's question and told the group of my problem and they embraced me. I'm pleased to say, with the help of men whom I love deeply, who care deeply about me and who hold me accountable, I am no longer controlled by the need to view porn. However, the recovery was by no means an overnight process and I realize I am always susceptible to falling back into it. That is the nature of addictions.

Control is important. When we lose control, we find we are hopelessly at odds with ourselves and, eventually, with others. Understanding what we can control and what we cannot control is important in our ability to respond appropriately to both. This simple understanding will provide us with a much greater sense of inner peace, which I think is best expressed by the Serenity Prayer:

> "God grant me the serenity to accept the things I cannot change, courage to change the things I can, and the wisdom to know the difference."

What is the difference between the things we can control and the things we cannot control? The answer is simple: If it's not you, you can't control it.

The only thing we can really control is ourselves. That's it. I can control only my thoughts, my speech, and my actions. I can't control what will happen to me, but I can have an influence on what happens to me based on my decisions and choices. This is why decision-making should be made from an informed position. Otherwise the probability of making a poor choice increases dramatically. As a boy, I responded to a traumatic loss by suppressing my feelings and emotions. It wasn't even a conscious choice – I just had no other information by which to act, so I did nothing. I was uninformed and, therefore, lacked opportunity to make an informed decision. My default coping mechanism was suppression of my feelings and emotions. I couldn't control the accident that took my brother's life, and I had no knowledge of how to deal with it. This resulted in my adoption of unhealthy coping mechanisms in a failed attempt to deal with the trauma. A few years later I found drugs and alcohol to have a numbing effect not only on my pain, but on my decision-making, core values and beliefs. As a result, I became addicted to pornography. I am a fortunate overcomer due to the influence of a loving wife and good men in my life. I emphasize the word influence only to make a point: Denise and these men, as loving and as good as they are, had no control over me – only influence. Thankfully, their influence was positive and I chose to embrace it.

What influence do the people in your life have on you? Is it positive? If so, embrace it. If you are surrounded by those whose influence is negative, reject it. It's your decision as to whom or what you allow to influence you. Negative choices will diminish self-control and positive choices will enhance it. In deciding what influence you will follow, the first choice will be between doing nothing and doing something. Doing nothing doesn't mean you've made a negative choice. In fact, doing nothing, depending upon the circumstances, may be your only positive choice. In many cases, the choice to do nothing demonstrates great patience and wisdom. Doing nothing for a period of time can actually bring clarity for the best course of action to take. This is why after a good night's sleep or after a meditative state we are able to think more clearly, be more decisive, and be less anxious. Doing nothing can give your brain a rest and allow time for variables over which you have no control to play out and provide clarity. Ultimately, the decision to act or not act based on the influencers in your life is in your control.

How We Treat Others

Something else you can control is your tongue. Sounds strange? In the Bible, James compares the tongue to a small rudder controlling the direction of a large ship and to a small spark capable of igniting a great forest fire. His point? Your words have great influence and should be tightly controlled. You can look at any divisive issue and immediately recognize the power of words. All you have to do is watch a few minutes of news or browse social media and you will see the power of words in political, religious, racial, and social issues. Let the "unfriending" begin! Negative, destructive, and divisive words inflict wounds that can destroy relationships or prevent them from developing. They can create a wide chasm between people which, over repeated instances, cannot be bridged.

Positive words, on the other hand, have exactly the opposite effect. When you exercise the control of your tongue to build up and encourage others, you draw them closer to you because they feel better about themselves when they're with you. This is known as the law of attraction and it can have amazing results. When you make the decision to be intentional in your encouragement of every person you encounter, regardless of how they treat you, you will see a change in them. With the stress and anxiety filling our lives, we all long for positive influences. Just as I spoke earlier of how we can be positively and negatively influenced, we can be either a positive or negative influence to others. When we positively influence others we make them feel better. People desire to be with others who make them feel better about themselves. They also tend to reciprocate this behavior. The law of attraction can change how people feel about themselves, how they think about others and how they act toward others. If you question the validity of this statement, let me introduce you to Derek Black and Matthew Stevenson.

Derek Black is a former White Nationalist. His father, Don Black, was a grand wizard of the Ku Klux Klan (KKK). His godfather and uncle was David Duke, a former Louisiana State Representative, white supremacist, white separatist, and a former grand wizard of the KKK. Derek was an heir apparent to become a grand wizard of the KKK and had every intention of doing so. In 2010 Derek enrolled in and started studies at a small liberal arts college in Florida where nobody knew of him or his beliefs. It was a safe place for him to hide his identity. Each morning he would call in to his father's talk show to express views and he would frequently post his comments and opinions to his father's website, named Stormfront. He enjoyed living in anonymity at his college while he continued to fuel the flames of hatred in his hometown. While in his first semester of college he became acquainted with a Jewish student, Matthew Stevenson, who, as it turned out, was already acquainted with him. Matthew was a person who was interested in those with opposing beliefs. He had seen some of the anti-Semitic posts made by Derek on Stormfront. He had private discussions with Derek, but never about White Nationalism. Matthew wanted Derek to know him as a human being, so he didn't let on to Derek that he knew who he was. He figured if he first confronted Derek about his anti-Semitic views, he would only create in Derek a need to defend himself rather than to learn about Matthew as a person. Instead, Matthew made the decision to be a friend rather than an adversary, and he never shared Derek's views or identity with others on campus.

Eventually, however, there were social activist students who found both the Stormfront website and the posts by Derek. Upon being discovered, he was essentially shunned on campus by every student organization and student ... except for Matthew. As much as he initially wanted to hate Matthew because of his race and religion, Derek found Matthew to be the only one to treat him with civility in spite of his White Nationalist views. Once Derek had been "outed," Matthew was willing to speak with Derek about his views. Derek found Matthew to be very intelligent and respectful in presenting Derek with a different perspective on humanity. Matthew believed in the value of all people and treated Derek with both dignity and respect, as was evidenced by the fact he would befriend someone with such animosity toward his entire race. Derek was drawn to Matthew because of the way Matthew made him feel. Matthew went so far as to invite Derek to observe a Friday night Shabbat dinner he regularly hosted in his dorm room. Matthew was intentional about inviting both Jewish and non-Jewish students to the dinners as a means of building community. His intent in making the invitation was not to change Derek's views, but to expose Derek to Jewish people and Jewish traditions. This way, when Derek made anti-Semitic comments, he would do so with a true knowledge of the people. However, over the next two to three years of conversations between Derek and Matthew, Derek's views changed. He saw the goodness in Matthew and realized the error in expressing hatred toward a race vs. being in relationship with a person. The beliefs of Derek's parents and grandparents, as it turns out, were baseless. Recognizing and acting on this truth set Derek free from the bonds of hatred. While there is serious tension between Derek and his old community, the mental oppression created within him due to hatred and false judgment are gone. The law of attraction can change how people feel about themselves, how they think about others, and how they act toward others.

How We Think

Have you ever stopped to think about what you think about? In the world of programming this would be called a "loop," which essentially arrests the function of the program … kind of like a technological mental paralysis. In the field of neurobiology, however, this is known as metacognition and it represents the highest level of thinking (at least to our knowledge) in all of creation. Our brain is a masterpiece over which we have been given complete control. When we are free from oppression, we have the ability not only to control our thoughts but to stop our thoughts and change our thoughts. Freedom of thought means we are open to receive information provided by other sources, analyze the accuracy and validity of the information, and change our belief system if warranted. An example is a young adolescent who makes the decision to start smoking in order to be accepted by a certain social group. After taking a few health classes and watching some documentaries on lung cancer and its effect on quality and length of life, this youth decides, perhaps, his original decision was a bad one – what guys might refer to as "stinkin' thinkin.'" It may have gotten them accepted, but this young person is now thinking beyond simply being accepted by a group and has changed his mind for longer term health reasons.

I've become an expert on stinkin' thinkin.' I remember morning drives in to work when I would be thinking about the previous day's disagreement with another employee. I would think to myself how close-minded the person was and how inconsiderate and dismissive they were with their comments related to my ideas. I would think about how unjust they were in their position and how they were constantly at odds with me. I would think about their evil motives and the opposition they probably set up against me and the things they were probably saying to other people about me. I would think about how they had no right to treat me the way they did. I would imagine telling them what I really think about them. I'd even anticipate what they would say back to me. I would escalate the issue and the argument with them in my own mind and suddenly realize … I have just created a story in my own mind to vilify this person and make myself a victim – and they haven't even been part of the conversation. I had to stop my thoughts … my stinkin' thinkin'.

We all do it. We create a story in our own mind to make ourselves look good or justified in our behaviors. The same story usually makes those who oppose us the evil villains. In such instances I would have to say to myself, sometimes out loud, "Stop it, Chris! The story you are telling yourself is not true!" I would then search my mind for any number of other reasons for the person's opposition and the validity of their position. This would allow me to go speak calmly to the other person about their perspective and gain greater insight to their position. Information and insight provide understanding and understanding adds clarity to our thought processes. Clarity in our thoughts allows us to be more adaptable and flexible to new thoughts and new beliefs. When our thoughts are more adaptive, our behaviors also become more adaptive and we behave differently toward others. We make them feel better about themselves and make them feel better about being with us. It all starts with how we think. Positive thoughts beget positive behaviors and results. Negative thoughts beget negative behaviors and results. It's all in our control!

Let's be honest, though. We don't always feel in control – because we're not. We have control over our thoughts, responses, and choices. We do not have control over others or everything happening around us. Sometimes the pain of feeling out of control, as I experienced after my brother's death, leads to addictions. Now it's your turn. I'm going to take you mentally into the committee room where we're all asked to reveal our addictions. If you have something currently controlling you, it's time for you to name it and take back control.

Summary Points of CONTROL

- Self-control and self-regulation help us to avoid feeling overwhelmed.
- Choices we make influence the control we take.
- Self-control is strengthened through accountability.
- We cannot control what others say or do ... we can only control ourselves and how we *respond* to what others say and do.
- We are influenced by others – choose who you surround yourself with wisely.
- You control your tongue – choose your words carefully.
- We have complete control over how we think and what we think about ... better control of our thoughts leads to better control of our behaviors.

Questions for Reflection

- What are the control issues you struggle with?
- What or who do you need to acknowledge is not in your control?
- How do you react to feeling out of control?
- How do you cope with feeling out of control?
- How do the people in your life influence you, either positively or negatively?

4

ADDICTION

John Featherston, a fifth-generation preacher and a good friend, wrote a book called *Never Alone Again*. It recounts his journey of faith and addiction as he dealt with the desire to influence change in the church, the pressure of pastoring a resistant congregation, falling from the grace of its membership, and finding his true calling into a new ministry of addiction recovery – Serenity Church. He welcomes all into his church every Saturday night with the same words ... "We're a fellowship for anybody who has something in your life that hurts you and that you can't just 'wish' or 'will' away. I believe that's every human being on the planet I've met so far."

For the purposes of this chapter, I'm dispensing with the clinical definition of addiction and aligning myself with John's definition. I'm doing this because, for most men, there is a personal, internal struggle we would like to "wish" or "will" out of our lives. It doesn't matter whether or not we are clinically dependent, developing a tolerance, or experiencing withdrawals. The pain we experience as a result of deep and personal struggle is real. I think this is something we can all agree on, so let's proceed based on John's observation: "I believe that's every human being on the planet I've met so far."

We all have addictions. They touch every life. Whether it's your own addiction or the addiction of a loved one causing you pain, the suffering is real. Addiction comes in many forms: drugs, alcohol, work, shopping, gambling, pornography, sex, gaming, thrill seeking, and power, to name a few.

I was offended at the idea that somebody would classify me as an addict, because I didn't consider myself one of "those people." I wasn't a guy who had failed in life, couldn't hold a job, or whose family hated him. I wasn't a guy who people disapproved of. I wasn't a drunk or a junkie. I had things under control … except for one thing only I knew about. It was this one thing, pornography (see Chapter 3, CONTROL), which hooked me. I thought it hurt no one – untrue. By viewing pornography, I was supporting human trafficking, sexual abuse, physical abuse and emotional abuse of many of those involved in the industry. I thought it would not affect me – untrue. The shame and guilt I bore for watching pornography affected my self-esteem. I thought it took nothing away from anyone else – untrue. Every minute of viewing pornography was a minute stolen from my family, my employer, or anyone else who relied on me or desired my time. I thought it would not affect me mentally – untrue. Pornography distorted my idea of healthy sexuality and intimacy. If there was any truth to the thought of pornography not causing me or others harm … why did I so desperately need to keep it a secret?

One of the most difficult aspects of addiction is keeping it a secret. There are three reasons people keep secrets. Two of them are bad. The good reason is to see the overwhelming joy of a person surprised with something meaningful and affirming. The first bad reason is to avoid punishment for something we should not have done. The second bad reason is to avoid the utter shame and embarrassment we feel when someone whose respect we desire realizes we've been deceptive - living a lie. I believe the most burdensome secret is the last one. The first bad reason for keeping a secret, to avoid punishment, is about self-preservation after making a poor choice. Everybody at some point in their life makes a poor choice for which they don't want to be held responsible. However, in most cases this choice doesn't have an ongoing effect on the life of the individual or those who love them. Obviously, there are also some more consequential choices, but the poor choices made by most of us are manageable despite their consequences. Addictions are the enduring secrets which, if not exposed and treated, become less manageable over time. They can take more of a personal toll on the individual - mentally, physically, emotionally and spiritually. Those close to the individual can likewise be affected by the deep hurt and erosion of trust accompanying the disclosure of a painful reality. A revealed addiction requires both the individual and those who care for them to deal with the loss of trust. It requires issues creating the need for emotional escape to be identified, processed and resolved. Dysfunctional coping (the addiction) serving as an escape must be eliminated and replaced with healthy coping mechanisms. The addicted person can emerge as the overcomer through this deep dive into cause and effect and through the support of others. The victim becomes victorious.

No one ever classified me as an addict or someone with a problem. I recognized it myself the first time I heard John Featherston define addiction as a cause of suffering and something we can't "wish" or "will" away. It was a remnant of the past pain of my life continuing to be internalized. Until I gained the courage to be honest about it with the person I cared for most, my wife, I would remain firmly in the grip of its talons. Being in the grip of addiction is a very lonely existence.

Whether addiction is acted out internally or externally, it has an isolating effect. I'm not talking about solitude. Solitude can be refreshing and enjoyable ... a time for introspection and growth. The feeling of being isolated and alone, however, can be experienced in different ways. For those who are healthy, feelings of loneliness can be experienced as a melancholy or sweet nostalgic moment from which we emerge with contentment, knowing it's temporary. For the addict, feeling alone brings no joy, hope, or contentment. It feels terrible and permanent. Loneliness, for the addict, is an unmet need to be in community with others – to be supported and encouraged. Isolation, loneliness, and sadness are but a few of the characteristics of depression. The presence of these characteristics within the addict is not uncommon. It is also not uncommon, in the face of these symptoms, for the addict to return to his or her addictive behaviors as a source of momentary escape from the pain, creating a continuing downward spiral. For the person who feels isolated there can be a sense of hopelessness from the belief they will never "belong." The higher the level of despair, the more isolated he or she becomes and the greater the need to find escape. Without the guidance, encouragement, and direction of trusted friends, sponsors, or professionals we're left to our own impulses or the dysfunctional coping skills we've developed. We become isolated from others, causing increased emotional pain for ourselves. Emotional pain leads to suffering. Suffering searches for an alternative. Many times, the chosen alternative is only a temporary distraction from our suffering. We need more and more distraction in our attempt to overcome the temporary nature of our relief. Too often this habit develops into addiction without ever going back to the source of the pain and dealing with it.

Connection

The opposite of addiction isn't sobriety, it's connection. Through connection we're emotionally fulfilled, while nothing fills the void of being disconnected. Power, wealth, and influence are not a substitute. They may appear to be, but they're more likely to result in pathology than connectivity. Addiction causes loneliness, shame, and despair. With treatment, addiction can be transitioned to sobriety – obviously a huge step in the right direction for returning to a healthier lifestyle. Being sober, however, is not the same as being connected. Being healthier is not enough – experiencing joy and quality of life is the ultimate goal. It's only a reachable goal when we've made meaningful connections with others, a Higher Power, or both. Through connection we find support, fulfillment, and higher purpose for our lives. You'll see this lived out in many strong 12-step communities – members who are supportive of each other and who seek to give back in some way to those who are struggling. Through strength of community they are able to transform their own struggles into a platform from which they can strengthen others who struggle.

Generally speaking, men are not good at seeking help. Men will bear the weight of most burdens independently and internally, thinking they have within themselves the means to overcome the problem. Some have high resilience and are successful in doing so. Others are resilient yet, for some reason, are ineffective in dealing with struggles. Their attempt to overcome their issues only generates more stress, more need for escape, and a higher likelihood of developing some form of self-medication to distract them from their own issues. This is why it is important to be connected. But this is contradictory to the cultural and societal messages delivered to men. We hear the old "men are hunters and women are gatherers" adage and our interpretation is that we have the sole responsibility for providing. We compound this errant thinking by believing this responsibility is to be exercised independently. This is not true today and never was. We need to be not only connected to others, but in community with others.

Community

If we look at how the hunt takes place in the natural setting we find it is done in community. Lions don't pursue prey alone. Hyenas don't pursue prey alone. Wolves don't pursue prey alone. The Native American hunters did not hunt alone. The way of nature is to function as a community.

What's the difference between connection and community? Let me use my own siblings as an example. I have three older sisters who live on the east coast and one older brother who lives in the west. I live in Texas. Although we are not part of the same community and don't have a chance to converse often, I am deeply connected to each of them every day on an emotional level. Together, through childhood and adolescence we experienced love, laughter, joy, sorrow, pain, and grief. Neither time nor distance can break the bond created over the course of our lives. A sense of connection is emotional. A sense of community is physical. Within my community are men with whom I meet regularly over coffee and friends with whom I worship. My community includes my family - my wife, children, and grandchildren with whom I celebrate life and give and receive support. Some refer to their community as their "tribe." I really like the feel of this because our tribal instincts are all about support, care, and protection of a group of people to whom we are committed and who are committed to us. Our tribe is also the members of our community with whom we are deeply connected.

If isolation is the enemy of the addict, a community of reliable and positively focused supporters is the ally. We only need to look at statistics of addiction for evidence of the negative effect the cultural and societal message promoting masculine independence is having on men. There are numerous studies and a great deal of research on the subject but, generally speaking, men are found to be twice as likely as women to develop an addiction to drugs and alcohol. When it comes to sex and pornography, men are three times more likely to develop addictions than women. Why are men at higher risk? Women are more likely to be in community with other women, to discuss their problems, to provide emotional support to each other, and to seek professional help. The tendency of men is to be "lone wolves" and, therefore, vulnerable. A lot of temptations can take us down. There are a lot of struggles and issues causing pain in our lives. This is true for each of us. You are not alone in your struggle. Take steps to find a community with whom you can connect.

What causes you pain that you can't wish or will away? What is it doing to you? Consider what is at stake if you don't gain control over it:

- Loss of family relationships

- Loss of a job (and possibly a career)

- Loss of reputation

- Loss of respect

- Loss of your physical health

- Loss of your mental health

- Loss of financial security

- Loss of friendships

- Loss of freedom

- Loss of life

What price are you or those you love paying as a result of this enemy? It doesn't have to be this way. Get connected. Find your community. Recovery is achievable. It is more than just overcoming a struggle. Recovery is about the restoration of joy, fulfillment, and quality of life.

Summary Points of ADDICTION

- You can't just "wish" or "will" addiction away.

- Addiction causes pain and suffering.

- Addictions are enduring secrets which, if not exposed and treated, become less manageable over time.

- Addiction is isolating.

- The opposite of addiction is not sobriety – it is connection.

- Consider what is at stake if you don't gain control over addiction.

- Recovery occurs in a connected community.

- The ultimate goal of recovery is more than sobriety – it is joy, fulfillment, and quality of life.

Questions for Reflection

- What behaviors, thoughts, or activities would you like to "wish" or "will" out of your life?

- What do they cause you to unintentionally support or neglect?

- Who do they unintentionally affect?

- Who in your community will you connect with to talk about your struggle?

5

COMMUNICATION

For the most part, men are not considered to be masters of communication. I'm looking for a word to more accurately describe the communication style of most men ...

I've got it! ... "Cave-dweller."

A little harsh? Here's the thing – effective communication involves more listening than speaking. It involves communicating purpose, feelings, and emotions. It involves clarity of message. It involves understanding intent, reading body language and knowing when a conversation is casual and when it is crucial. It involves knowing whether silence is helpful or harmful. It involves proper judgment of the situation and environment. It involves knowing who to talk to and who not to talk to. How are you doing so far, men?

I am a lifelong student of communication. We all are. We begin learning about communication before we're even born. We sense and recognize certain sounds and vibrations. It might be music, it might be a barking dog, or it might be the voice of our mother. Whatever we hear in the womb captures our attention in some manner and our brain records and stores it. This mental recording and storing of information continues for the rest of our life.

As the youngest in a family of six children, I learned to communicate largely through observation, messaging I received, and my interpretation of that messaging (the story I learned to tell myself). Being the last child in a large family, I learned to follow. Born of parents whom I believe to be introverts by nature, I was fairly quiet. As a child I also had a slight speech impediment – a lisp – for which I went to speech therapy. These environmental, biological, and physiological factors created in me a tendency to be more comfortable observing and listening than speaking. Although this basic tendency has never changed, I learned as I grew older to adapt to my environment as needed and became more comfortable and confident in my communication ability. Whether you are a born introvert or extrovert; whether you are the first, last, or only child; whether you have any form of impediment or not … to survive and succeed in any area of your life you must interact effectively.

As a counselor, the main deficiency I see in men is an inability to communicate feelings effectively. But we weren't born this way. We have been trained this way – to our own detriment. The meanest things said between young boys (in addition to demeaning young girls) were words like: "You run like a girl," "You throw like a girl," "You cry like a girl," "You're a wuss," etc. Get the picture? We've been trained, generation after generation, to act like a man and not show emotions. Men who come into my office are sometimes overcome by years of bottled up emotions. They feel the need to apologize … to apologize! … for crying. For the sake of good communication, we've got to dispel the notion that expression of feelings and emotions is a bad thing. Effective communication of feelings and emotions is the starting point for all effective communication.

Thoughts are often confused with feelings and emotions. For instance, when I ask a man in a counseling session to tell me how he feels about something, his response will most likely start with the words "I think." We are trained not to feel, therefore we have learned to repress feelings and express thoughts. The thoughts we express are often going to be influenced by our expectation of what others want to hear. A detour has been wired within our brains to completely avoid the rough road of feelings and remain at all times on the paved and most traveled road of societal thinking. A great technique for expression of feelings I learned from Dr. Les Parrot at a conference in Dallas is what he refers to as the XYZ formula. It can be used to express positive feelings to affirm others and it can be used to express negative feelings in a non-threatening and non-blaming way. It goes like this:

In situation **X**
When you did/said **Y**
I felt **Z**

Here is how it might look in an affirming statement used at work:

In our staff meeting (**X**)
when you said you valued my opinion (**Y**)
I felt appreciated and respected (**Z**)

Here is how it might look in expressing a negative feeling at work:

When you invited me to lunch with your investors (**X**)
and you didn't introduce me to anyone (**Y**)
I felt ignored and isolated (**Z**)

As guys, we might read the first example of an affirmation and think, "Well, it's good to thank people who support and acknowledge you." On the other hand we might read the second example and say, "Look, quit complaining. Put your big boy pants on and introduce yourself next time." This is the expectation – express thanks for the good and shut up about the bad. Here's the deal with that expectation – it's not healthy. It's not healthy at work and it's not healthy at home. It leads to repressed feelings which leads to resentment which leads to anger which leads, over time, to broken relationships. When we use the XYZ formula we are not blaming others for our feelings. We are taking ownership of our feelings because it is, after all, our choice to be offended or not be offended. We don't say "you made me feel." We say "I felt" and we name the situation. If we can identify the feeling we experienced (and own it) and the situation in which we experienced it, we will be much more successful in calmly communicating this feeling. When it comes to remaining calm in sensitive conversations, one of the most effective resources I have come across is the book *Crucial Conversations – Tools for Talking When Stakes Are High*, authored by Patterson, Grenny, McMillan and Switzler. If you haven't read it, I suggest you do so. I refer to it often in the work I do with nearly all of my clients because ineffective communication is central to, or at least a part of, what creates dysfunction in many of their lives.

The basic premise of making a crucial conversation successful, according to the authors, is to "Start with the Heart." You cannot control or change others. You can only control or change yourself. You are responsible for what you say and how you respond. It will be helpful to inspect your heart and ask yourself the following three questions before the conversation begins:

1. What result do I want for myself?

2. What result do I want for the other person?

3. What result do I want for this relationship?

Remember … if it's not good for both parties, it's not good for the relationship, and if it's not good for the relationship, it's not good for either party. In other words, a "my way or the highway" approach won't work. If your heart is in the right place, your response to all of these questions will be benevolent. If that's the case, you're ready to begin the conversation. During the conversation you'll need to check your attitude and behavior from time to time with this follow-up question:

If I've been honest in my answer to the three questions above, am I behaving in a way consistent with those responses?

If you get good at this you should have a miraculous transformation in communications, right? Wouldn't this be nice – but no. The human brain is much too complex for it to be that easy. Our brains sense in others their body language, physiological signs (red in the face, rapid movement, facial expression, etc.), emotions, and behaviors. All of these cues inform us regarding the other person's comfort level with the conversation. We also have the ability to be aware of our own non-verbal cues to recognize whether we are feeling safe or unsafe in a conversation. To communicate effectively we must learn to detect the emotions of others and be aware of our own emotions. Through this awareness we will know when the timing for certain discussions is right.

I started the chapter with the statement "effective communication involves more listening than speaking." As a counselor, I'm a paid listener. My professional purpose is to listen closely for understanding. This means listening to tone, "listening" to body movement, listening to what is said and what is not said, listening for feelings and emotions, listening for consistency between thoughts and actions, listening without judgment or condemnation, and listening with a 100% focus on my clients. If you think it's a waste of time and money to pay someone to listen, let me ask you … does anyone else go to this level of listening with you? Do you go to this level of listening with anyone else? Most people simply listen to respond. For many guys the only purpose in listening is to respond, not to understand. We want to provide a solution, express agreement or disagreement, defend a position, or answer with the brevity required to simply stop the discussion. Some guys, like me, learn the difference between hearing and listening the hard way. I remember sitting in my recliner and watching a football game one Saturday afternoon when Denise began talking to me. I heard her, but only pretended to listen. I continued to focus on the game, wishing all the while she would stop talking so I could pay attention to what was really important. She went on for several minutes, her voice fading into the white noise of my mind … until her last three words: "Don't you agree?" Uh oh.

We need to learn to listen. We need to learn to listen not to respond, but to understand. An exercise I do with couples is to have one person talk about a struggle they're experiencing and how it makes them feel. The other person's job is to listen, not interrupt, and then to repeat back to the person speaking what was said and expressed. Here's how it generally goes when a man (let's call him Boudreaux) speaks and a woman (let's call her Wynonna) listens:

Boudreaux: I'm struggling with my tractor. It's broke. I'm tryin' to fix it.

(Silence)

Counselor: And how does that make you feel?

Boudreaux: It's hot outside. It makes me feel hot.

Counselor: Thank you for sharing, Boudreaux. Wynonna, can you tell me what you heard Boudreaux say and express?

Wynonna: I heard Boudreaux say he was tired of struggling with that damned ol' tractor of his and that it was hot outside. He felt hot.

Counselor: Boudreaux, would you say Wynonna properly summed up your struggle and feelings?

Boudreaux: Yep.

Here's how it generally goes when a woman speaks and a man listens:

Wynonna: Well … this might seem petty of me, but Boudreaux and I had planned to go to the Farmer's Market Saturday morning and I was really looking forward to our time together. But a friend of his called early that morning to invite him hunting and he went with his friend instead of spending time with me. I just felt like I didn't mean as much to him. After they hunted he called to tell me they were going out for something to eat and to have a few drinks. I was pretty upset but he didn't seem to understand why. I asked him what he expected me to do alone all day without him. I got so irritated with him I finally said, "Fine … I guess I'll just stay home alone and do all the chores we were going to work on together." Then I hung up on him. I didn't hear back from him and he ended up not coming home until about 11:00 at night. He wasn't in good shape. I was angry, so I wouldn't speak to him that night. I wound up going to church alone on Sunday morning and then eating lunch alone when I got home. He had gotten up late and went out to work on his tractor. We really didn't speak much that day. I just felt alone and unappreciated.

Counselor: Thank you for sharing, Wynonna. Boudreaux, can you tell me what you heard Wynonna say and express?

Boudreaux: She doesn't like chores.

Counselor: Wynonna, would you say Boudreaux properly summed up your struggle and feelings?

Wynonna: No.

Counselor: Can you tell me what he missed?

Wynonna: Boudreaux! Were you even listening to me?!?!?

(Boudreaux looks abnormally bewildered.)

Counselor: Wynonna, would you summarize what you said for Boudreaux?

Wynonna: Damn right I will! *I said:* I was looking forward to going to the Farmer's Market with him, as we had planned, on Saturday morning! *I said:* It bothered me that, instead, he took a call from a friend who invited him quail hunting and he went! *I said:* Afterwards, he and the group of guys went out drinking and he came stumbling home drunk at 11:00 that night! *I said:* I wouldn't speak to him that night. *I said:* After going to church ALONE on Sunday morning I came home and ate lunch ALONE while he worked on his damn tractor! *I said:* I felt alone and unimportant to him. *I said:* He must have assumed I would be fine being home by myself doing chores all day when there is way too much for any person to do alone!

Counselor: Thank you, Wynonna. Boudreaux, can you tell me how Wynonna feels?

Boudreaux: Angry?

Counselor: Good, Boudreaux. She expressed some other feelings which we'll discuss as well, but you've done a good job of listening to her tone. Why would you say she's angry?

Boudreaux: Because she didn't get the chores done?

We can laugh this off because poor ol' Boudreaux is so clueless. But if we're honest, we can substitute John, Sam, Steve, Mark, Paul, Rick, David, Bill, Scott, Chris, or any other name into this script, knowing we've all experienced a serious failure to understand because we weren't listening properly.

Attitudes that Prevent Listening

There are several attitudes we can have while listening to others which potentially prevent us from understanding what is being communicated. Here's a clue about your attitude of listening: Observe your own body language. Effective and active listening means (in American culture) you are making eye contact. It means you are facing the person speaking to you. It means you have put down whatever else you were doing. You are giving full and sole attention to hear what is said. Turn off the TV. Put down your book. Stop what you are working on. Failure to do these things immediately tells your partner you are not engaged with them. Once we have the physical aspect of listening addressed, we want to check the mental aspect. Here are a handful of listening attitudes affecting our ability to gain understanding when we're spoken to:

"The need to fix" listening is common for guys. We feel like someone is coming for advice every time they present us with an issue. We jump right to "Here's what I would do…" or "Have you considered…?" or "You just need to … " When we do this we're making an assumption of our partner's needs which may be incorrect. Our partner will often tell us how they are feeling or what they are experiencing with the sole need of being heard – not to get a "fix." We need to allow them to express what is on their mind and not respond immediately. As uncomfortable as it may seem at first, allow yourself to sit in silence with someone who has presented a struggle. This gives both you and them time to process what they have said. They may discover there is more for them to express before you start speaking. If and when the time for you to respond arises, a more appropriate response is to ask the question: "I understand. Is there anything you would like me to do for you?" I've actually asked Denise this question before and was told there is nothing for me to do – she just needed to talk about what was on her mind. No need for a fix.

"I'm right – you're wrong" listening is an infirmity many of us suffer from. This is especially true when it comes to discussion of race, sex, gender, religion, or politics. We see the rigidity with which we and others state our positions on social media and on television programming every day. The polarization of society in recent years has become a phenomenon of technology making itself right at home in eroding our relationships. There is an element of control we find in this attitude of listening. If we acknowledge the potential validity of opposing views, the foundational beliefs on which we've built our house of cards may crumble. We would lose control over the beliefs with which we're comfortable. The better option is to listen to all views with respect for the foundational beliefs of others. Once you've done this, each of you can process the opposing views and, if necessary, adjust your own views as you deem appropriate. It's possible there can be more than one valid point of view. If neither of you believe it's appropriate to change your position after honestly considering the other's perspective, agree to disagree and move on.

"It's not my fault" listening means we're more interested in assigning blame than we are in listening to the other person's point or perspective. Honestly, this is a form of listening indicative of insecurity – insecurity not visible to others but deep-seated within us. If you find your inner voice saying "it's your fault" or "it's their fault" to someone speaking to you, check yourself. Why is there a need to assign blame? Are you taking responsibility for your own part in a misunderstanding? Is it possible there are certain conditions over which no one person had control? If we habitually blame others for misunderstandings or failures of some nature, people start to wonder why we always find someone else to blame. They begin to notice our repetitive pattern of blaming others and we become less credible. You can probably think of one of these types of listeners as you're reading this. If so, you have confirmation of how noticeable and annoying this style of response can be.

The **"everybody is out to get me"** listener is, quite frankly, hard to take. The world is always against them and there seems to be a neediness for attention or consoling. People quickly lose patience with this. In its most severe form the person comes off as being paranoid or some sort of conspiracy theorist. No matter what you say to this kind of listener they will reverse the attention back on to themselves and tell you a tale of their personal victimization.

"Resistant listening" occurs when a person believes, correctly or mistakenly, there is an attempt by the speaker to control them in some way. A resistant listener feels the other person is trying to manipulate and to take advantage of them. This listening attitude may be developed by someone who has been victimized, hurt, or otherwise wronged by someone in their past. There is an element of mistrust in their listening which can act as a barrier to recognizing genuineness in the person they are speaking with. The thought "I will not be controlled or manipulated so I can't be hurt again" protects this person from repeatedly being victimized but can also prevent them from seeing goodness and genuineness in others. If you've been manipulated in the past, it's reasonable to be wary of what people say to you – but realize there are also many trustworthy people out there who are not trying to control or take advantage of you in any way.

A **"selfish listener"** has a lot to overcome. Selfish listening simply means you tune out anything you don't want to do, believe, or agree with. Do you remember the three questions presented earlier in the chapter?

1. What result do I want for myself?

2. What result do I want for the other person?

3. What result do I want for this relationship?

Your verbal communications as well as your listening attitude need to reflect upon these three questions no matter what type of a relationship you are dealing with. We have to move beyond our own desires when we are listening to others. We must move beyond our own resistance and strike a balance between what we want and what others want. In doing so, we focus on what is good and healthy for the individuals as well as the relationship.

So far, a lot of these listening attitudes include a degree of self-deception. This disabling rigidity prevents the listener from seeing the possible validity and legitimacy of another person's perspective. It almost appears they have blinders on and are incapable of seeing a bigger picture – a larger and more informed view of the situation. In this self-deception, they can become defensive in an effort to protect their existing views and beliefs rather than expand them. At worst, they can become demanding and accusatory. Demanding in the sense they will try to mute the voices of others so they can be heard. Accusatory in the sense others are suspected of having a biased agenda and no true desire to hear their position. We see this demanding, self-deceptive, defensive and accusatory positioning most often in social media posts or discussions centered around the subjects of politics, religion, race relations, gender biases, and sexual identity biases. Too often, we cannot listen to what another person is saying because we're yelling too loud to hear. In fact, it's a rarity for any "listening" to occur on social media. On the other hand, it is a beautiful thing to watch two people with emotional and intellectual maturity discuss any of these issues because views expressed from either side are recognized by the other as a construct of their learned values and beliefs. To discuss the validity, or lack thereof, of any values and beliefs is a healthy thing to do for growth and understanding. We can listen for content and ask questions for clarity. We can then make the choice to amend or retain our own views. This decision can be made without vilifying the other person when we recognize their views are part of their value and belief system, a construct highly influenced by their environment. Regardless of whether or not you agree with someone, if you want their respect, listen to them.

Listening for Understanding

It's important to understand and respect each other, not necessarily to agree with each other. When we speak of listening it's important to recognize the difference between listening to understand and listening to respond. I can listen to someone to understand how they came to believe what they believe. This is about becoming aware of the construct of their values and beliefs previously discussed. This leads me to knowledge of their learned thoughts and behaviors. It does not require my agreement with them. If a member of the KKK explains to me how his or her understanding of Christianity supports the beliefs and values reinforced by those around them, I can understand how they came to believe what they believe. I absolutely disagree with it. If I want them to listen to my understanding of Christianity and how it supports my values and beliefs, I need to give them the respect of listening to theirs. My hope would be, through dialogue and through my own behaviors, they might grow to not only understand me, but to find themselves in agreement with me. But it starts with showing respect for the person, regardless of their ideology. It happens through relationship – one-on-one relationship. This is obviously a somewhat inflammatory example to make a point. What if we start with something much simpler – the one-on-one relationship you have with a spouse or partner. You may have differing ideas of the perfect vacation. You may have different ideas on parenting. You may have different ideas on spirituality and spiritual practices. You may disagree on certain groups of friends. Listen. Ask questions. Try to understand. Don't come into a discussion with the weaponry of a bad attitude. Don't come to the conversation armed to respond without considering the other person feels very deeply about their position for very good reason. Listen to understand, not to respond. I've heard when something is said three times, we need to pay attention to it. For this reason, I repeat the need to increase understanding for what is important to the relationship by asking yourself these questions:

1. What result do I want for myself?

2. What result do I want for the other person?

3. What result do I want for this relationship?

Listen to understand and always be respectful of the other person, even if you don't respect their views.

The Flow of Communication

Good communication feels smooth and easy. We don't allow ourselves to get wrapped around the axle over who "wins." Even in discussions with the potential to be emotionally charged, we don't allow argument to replace dialogue. Consider a healthy conversation to be like a couple dancing in perfect synchronization:

In Synchronized Dance	In Healthy Conversation
There is a lot of practice.	There is a lot of practice.
A time is set.	A time is set.
There is an invitation.	There is an invitation.
There is time for preparation.	There is time for preparation.
There is no forced movement.	No one feels controlled.
There is flow of movement.	Listening and speaking flows.
There is no stepping on toes.	There is no cutting off.
There is no ad libbing.	There is no deflecting.
There is relaxation.	There is calm.
There is constant connection.	There is understanding.
There is trust.	There is trust.
There is satisfaction.	There is satisfaction.
There is equal responsibility.	There is equal responsibility.

Effective conversation, like a smooth dance, takes a lot of work and it also involves knowing when to take a break. Sometimes we realize it's just not happening and we each have to separate for a brief period to collect our thoughts, refocus on purpose, and return to work with each other. No one quits.

Good communication requires you to share how you feel and say what you need - the people you need to communicate with are no better at mind-reading than you are. You don't need stress and tension poured into your life and relationships due to poor communication. It's time to crawl out of our caves and learn to communicate without being afraid of expressing our feelings.

Summary Points of COMMUNICATION

- Communication involves as much listening as speaking.

- Communication involves expression of purpose, feelings, and emotions.

- Communication involves understanding of: intent, body language, silence, and the environment.

- The XYZ formula helps in safely sharing and responding to both positive and negative feelings.

- In a crucial conversation, inspect your heart before you start. Ask: What result do I want for myself? What result do I want for the other person? What result do I want for this relationship?

- Check for safety – observe your own tone and physical cues as well as those of others in the conversation.

- Know when to take a timeout.

- Don't let a timeout turn into avoidance – return to the discussion with a fresh perspective after a calming down period.

- Pay attention to the attitude with which you are listening.

- Listen to understand, not to respond.

- Don't allow argument to replace dialogue.

- Share how you feel and say what you need.

Questions for Reflection

- How effective are you in communicating your feelings?

- How does environment and timing usually play into the effectiveness of your communications?

- Talk about a time when you were either attentive or inattentive to unspoken communication.

- Do you listen to understand, or do you listen to respond?

- How does your "listening attitude" prevent or promote understanding?

- When positions or opinions differ, do you normally find yourself trying to win an argument, or do you find yourself trying to create dialogue?

6

FEAR

What are you afraid of?

Men don't like this question. If you glossed over it in hopes of detouring around it … C'mon, man! Please pause for a minute and let this question marinate. Hold off on reading further until you've arrived at an answer. Hint: the only wrong answer is "Nothing."

What are you afraid of?

My fear is not being good enough. This means I worry about people judging me to be either average or below average. I have a tendency toward perfectionism which is probably both genetic and learned. I don't know if either of my parents were perfectionists, but my guess is, to a degree, one or both of them were. As I mentioned previously, I was the youngest of six children and, my hunch is, I learned excelling at something was a good way for me to get attention. It didn't matter if it was reading, writing, humor, or sports … I wanted to excel. My brother, Steve, and sister, Kathy, are the ones who excelled in academics. My sisters Trish and Jude cornered the market for creativity. I knew I couldn't compete in those arenas. A little brother has to know his limitations! As it turns out, I found my expertise to be in the written language. It served me well in school assignments, professional communications, contracts, and ultimately, in stringing enough thoughts into paragraphs to create the chapters you're now reading.

I learned I wanted to excel in something so I would stand apart from others. We're no longer hunters and gatherers. We find different ways to survive in this post-modern world. We develop and hone the skills earning us a higher spot on the ladder. In highly competitive academic and professional settings we're taught it's not good enough to be average. We learn we can only differentiate ourselves if we're above average. But I have a few questions about this: Can everybody be above average? Obviously not. Don't we need average people doing average things for all of our created systems to work? We absolutely do! Average is expected. Average is fine. Average is good. This is not to say each of us should not try our absolute best and consistently work toward improving ourselves. Yet, as men, we too often receive the message that average equals failure to excel. What is excellent is to do your best work and not compare yourself to others. What I have learned, and what I hope you will learn, is this: average is good and no one is perfect.

Fear comes in many forms and can be paralyzing if we're unable to separate rational fears from irrational fears. A lot of things can create fear in us. The following are fears I think most men can identify with. See if any of these might strike a chord with you:

Fear of Rejection

Can you remember your first crush? I remember mine. We met in sixth grade. She was pretty, outgoing, athletic, fun to be around, and very popular. I'm sure it would be okay to mention her name here because she'll probably never read this book, but we are Facebook friends now and word would probably get out. Come to think of it, I kind of like not mentioning her name here. I like the idea of all the girls from my middle school who are now Facebook friends wondering if it was them! Is that wrong?

I'll tell you what's wrong ... she *rejected* me! (I'm obviously still not quite over it.) When I asked if she would be my girlfriend, she graciously told me she was already dating a boy. I was unaware of that (an early reconnaissance failure), probably because "dating" in junior high simply means a boy and a girl talk. Even so, I was hurt and embarrassed by the rejection. What would you guess were the thoughts going through my mind when I had my next crush? "She's probably already dating someone," and "She might be out of my league." Rather than get hurt and embarrassed again it was easier not to ask my next crush to "date" me. I allowed the impact of one rejection to prevent me from asking someone else. This was obviously emotional and irrational on my part, but you can say that of many decisions made by preadolescents and adolescents.

Let's talk about rejection in more current and serious terms. You may be dealing with rejection from a desired school or job or promotion. You may be dealing with rejection from your siblings, your parents, your partner, or your children.

In the case of rejection related to school or vocation, it can actually have a positive effect. It can serve to motivate us. Some men have the ability to increase pressure in the face of rejection. That is to say they become more determined, work harder, work smarter, seek their own change, etc. This is a healthy mindset because they refuse to let rejection define them. For others, rejection can be so painful they decide to quit. They accept their circumstance as their "lot in life" and remain in a situation devoid of satisfaction, purpose, or meaning. Remaining in these circumstances can breed resentment, discord and, even worse, a sense of helplessness. At some point in life we all get knocked down. Perhaps multiple times. It's important not to allow rejection to keep us down. If you've experienced this type of rejection and are unsatisfied with the hand you've been dealt, remember you cannot change or control anyone else. You can only change yourself and how you respond. The change can only come from within you. If you don't like the hand you've been dealt, it's up to you to learn how to play the game better or change the game you're playing. This is all well and fine when we're talking about the pursuit of academics or pursuit of a career. But what about rejection from family?

We all long to belong. For most of us, family is the first group and the most important group to accept, support, and encourage us. Unfortunately, sometimes parents, children, siblings, or all of these become estranged over time. It might be a result of events in childhood such as emotional neglect, another form of abuse, or many other reasons. It might occur in adulthood due to failure to communicate effectively, failure to compromise, selfishness, or greed. Whatever the reason – if we're honest about it – estrangement hurts. Some will mask the hurt by saying "it's just as well," but most would like the relationship repaired if it could be. If you find yourself rejected by family (and your family might include your friends) and are feeling isolated, let me suggest you confront your feelings. Feelings of pain, anger, and hurt are important to discuss. Unaddressed, they can lead to deep resentment and an inability to forgive. Bitterness and blame can become deeply rooted within our thoughts and affect our ability to trust. If it is healthy for both parties, discussion and reconciliation can be attempted. If reconciliation is not advisable or possible due to safety reasons, reaching your own acceptance and contentment with the end of a relationship may be the healthiest course. When our sole focus is to find blame in others or ourselves, dealing with a problem is difficult. Instead, our attempt should be to seek understanding. If attempting reconciliation, the understanding we seek needs to be an understanding of the other person's perspective, not our own – we can already understand, justify, and defend our own perspective. The understanding I'm speaking of involves having compassion and empathy for the other person, allowing common ground to be found. You can't do this alone. All parties must be willing to lay their weapons down and remove their armor for reconciliation. Sometimes pride prevents this and sometimes vulnerability prevents it.

My best friend in high school was also the best man at my wedding. He was like a part of me. We did everything together – much of which we shouldn't have done! After the wedding we both got busy and we were living in separate cities. I missed seeing him a lot. After a year, I called to see if I could come and spend a weekend with him. We planned the date and I looked forward to it with every approaching day. I anticipated the fun we would have and the things we would discuss. When I arrived, I learned his older brother was also visiting from out of town and would also be spending the weekend with us. To make a long story short, I felt like a third wheel throughout the weekend and ended up resenting my friend instead of enjoying time with him. Rather than saying something, I chose to avoid conflict. I made the three hour drive home feeling rejected and increasingly irritated with each passing mile. Still, I chose not to discuss my anger with him. Several days went by and my anger subsided but my resentment and the feeling of rejection remained.

As men we're trained not to be needy, but there's no denying we are. The issue is not "if" we are needy, but "what" is our need. My need was to feel important and I didn't. This was on me, not my friend. I didn't feel important because my selfish expectation, which I didn't communicate to him, was not met. I'm sure he thought it would be "cool" for the three of us to be together, but I wanted his sole attention for the weekend and I didn't receive it. Even as I write this – thirty-five years later - I find it embarrassing to admit. I'm not supposed to be needy. I felt rejected. As a result, I rejected him.

I hope you don't have an embarrassing story like mine. But if you're a man I suspect you do, and perhaps you're the only one who knows it. Have you felt rejected by family or friends and, in return, rejected them? How long has it been since you've spoken? If you want to feel a sense of closure or a sense of wholeness, lay down whatever weapon you've been holding and whatever armor you've been using to protect yourself and seek reconciliation. Otherwise, rejection becomes loss.

Fear of Loss

Avoiding conflict, I didn't call my friend for weeks, which turned into months, which, embarrassingly, turned into years. I no longer carried resentment toward him or thought about rejection because I had moved on with my life. I was too busy with my work, family, and activities to continue with my immature response to that weekend so long ago. Rather than resentful, I was now embarrassed and ashamed of my pettiness – too embarrassed and ashamed to call him and admit my childish behavior. Years went by. I completely lost track of him and didn't know how to reach him even if I'd wanted to. I didn't know what city or country he lived in. I didn't know if he was married or if he had children. I actually didn't even know if he was still alive. But one day I was thinking about him and I had a new feeling – a sense of loss. I realized, because of my pride and my sense of righteous indignation over the years, I had lost something very valuable to me. I lost my best friend. I feared rejection, lived into the feeling of rejection and as a result experienced loss. I lost what I had and I lost what could have been. Older now, I realized my foolishness and looked up his parents. I called them to get his number. They were overjoyed to hear my voice and to learn about my life. That's when I knew this was the right thing to do, and long overdue. I called my friend and apologized for my pettiness. He was very gracious and realized both of us had gotten very busy. We caught up with each other's lives and wished each other well. This isn't a storybook ending where we vowed to get together each year and live happily ever after. In fact, that was probably about ten years ago and we haven't spoken since – but that's okay because we each had closure. I think of him fondly and once again enjoy the memories of the time we spent together. The loss of a friend is painful, but there are far more serious losses – loss of committed relationships, loss of a job, the death of a loved one, loss of sense of security and stability, or the loss of health. I have a few questions for you:

- What do you fear losing and why?

- How would your sense of self-worth change without it?

- How would you identify yourself if it is no longer part of your life?

- Would the loss paralyze you or allow you to move on and start living again and/or experience life more fully?

- If it's in your control, is there something different you should be doing today to protect against the loss?

These are difficult questions to answer, especially if what you fear losing is a relationship. Fear of loss can change our behavior if we're desperately trying to hold on. Some behavioral changes may be positive and helpful in our ability to move on and others may be negative and a hindrance. Dealing with the fear of loss is not easy, but it's even harder if you're doing it alone. Consider speaking with a friend or professional to process your fear or loss if it's negatively affecting your behavior, your life, or the lives of those around you. Don't be embarrassed to seek help, because we all need it and we all deal with fears and losses. They can be paralyzing but, with help, you can grow stronger and experience a return to joy. I know this. I am living proof of it. It's okay to experience fear of loss. Sometimes it's absolutely valid, but paralysis due to fear of loss or actual loss doesn't have to be permanent.

Any way we look at it, loss is tough. Whether it's the loss of friendship, loss of a marriage, loss of a job, or loss due to a death – it's tough. There's a process for closure and grieving we must allow. It's different for every one of us. We fear loss because there's a pain we feel and a wound to heal. I've heard it said: when tears of pain over a loss become tears of laughter over a memory, we are navigating the grief process well. Even though we fear the pain of loss, it's comforting to know we recover and don't have to live in it. We are resilient creations that, if we allow it, can be fully restored and move forward into joy-filled lives - not regretting loss, but growing from it. Viktor Frankl, an Austrian psychiatrist and Holocaust survivor, spoke to this beautiful truth in his book *Man's Search for Meaning*:

> "... often it is such a difficult external situation which gives man opportunity to grow spiritually beyond himself."

Fear of Insignificance

Friedrich Nietzsche, German philosopher, said, "He who has a why to live for can bear almost any how."

When we ask "why?" we're asking "what is the purpose?" When we search for the purpose in our own lives, we're attempting, to the best of our ability, to discover life's meaning. While each of us, depending upon our worldview, spiritual beliefs, etc., may come up with a different answer, all of our answers will be rooted in one common desire – significance.

Just as desire for significance is common to all men, so is the fear of insignificance. We want to leave a mark. We want to have an impact. It doesn't have to be large, just significant. Sometimes we mistake the two for being the same. Significance comes in all forms and sizes. Martin Luther King, Jr. was significant in his impact on the world due to his passion for civil rights. My daughter, Stephanie, and her husband, Alex, are having a significant impact on the lives of their daughter and son due to their passion for them to grow and mature into healthy, intelligent, and selfless adults. MLK, Jr. has impacted the world and Stephanie and Alex are impacting their children. Does one have more significance than the other? If your answer is yes, let me reframe the idea of significance in how we raise our children.

Martin Luther King, Jr. was raised by his father, MLK, Sr. and his mother, Alberta Williams King. MLK, Sr. was an activist and preacher in the African American district of Atlanta. He would teach his son of political matters and social justice. He sent his son to work in the fields to teach him respect for his ancestors. His mother nurtured him in his faith and instilled in him a sense of dignity and significance. Martin Luther King, Jr. said of his father:

> "I guess the influence of my father also had a great deal to do with my going into the ministry. This is not to say that he ever spoke to me in terms of being a minister, but that my admiration for him was the great moving factor. He set forth a noble example that I didn't mind following."

Martin Luther King, Jr's parents raised their son out of a motivation for him to grow and mature into a healthy, intelligent, and selfless adult. They were not famous nor do we hear much about them, because they stand in his shadow. It would be fair and correct to say MLK, Jr's parents had a significant impact on their child and, therefore, on the world. Stephanie and Alex are having a significant impact on their children and their children will carry the legacy of this impact forward in their lives and for generations to come. No impact is insignificant.

Our culture and society unfortunately equate significance with power, wealth, and corporate value. A good friend of mine was an associate director for a major communications company for nearly fifteen years. This is a man whose character and integrity are unquestionable and whose contributions to the organization were, according to his co-workers and supervisors, significant. Regardless, on a winter day in 2018, he received a letter from the Human Resources department advising his position was now considered "non-essential."

Non-essential.

Just let that burn into your gut for a minute. Can you imagine what this does to a man's self-esteem? Can you relate to how it affects his understanding of his own professional identity and worth? After this event he and I met over coffee nearly every week to discuss his direction, his purpose and, as a man of deep faith, God's purpose for his life. What we discovered together goes back to the question we began with ... why? What was the purpose in this? Unsurprisingly, the answer came to him by leaning into his faith. We journeyed together through questions of purpose, values, fears, family, life balance, and significance. He discovered, despite his effectiveness in his corporate job and the significant contribution he made to not only the organization but the people within it, God had been preparing him for more and had a greater purpose for him.

Years before, he had returned to school to get a Master's Degree in Counseling and, since then, had been mentoring and coaching individuals and couples through various struggles in whatever spare time he had. He discovered, while he was very good at his job, his greater significance was his relationship with people. This realization led him to abandon his corporate pursuits entirely and to enter the field of professional counseling full time. Through our countless discussions over coffee, something became clear to both of us: significance is not measured by power, wealth, profits, or corporate success. Significance is measured by relationships and the impact we have on people's lives. It doesn't matter if your impact is global, generational, or individual – your significance is born through relationship.

If you fear insignificance, take a look at your relationships. Consider your friendships of the past and present. Consider your family – past, present, or future – and you will know you are significant. If you are estranged from loved ones, no matter their relationship to you, reach out. Your effort to enter into or to restore a relationship is, in itself, significant. If you are still struggling with significance, I encourage you to go back to Chapter 1, EXPLORING VALUES, and see if perhaps there is misalignment between your core values and your understanding of significance.

Fear of Vulnerability

Weakness.

This word, either consciously or subconsciously, goes through the mind of most men when they hear the word vulnerable. From an early age, we're taught "boys don't cry." We're told to "suck it up." We're required to be strong. If we fail to meet masculine expectations, we're told we are soft. Because of this, men associate vulnerability with weakness. Having been in the corporate world for thirty-five years, I understand the reality of business, competitive markets, and the need to appear as the strongest in your area of expertise. I also understand the toll it takes on men and their loved ones when there is not an outlet for honest expression of feelings of vulnerability.

Realistically, the workplace may not be an environment where vulnerability can be shown on a regular basis. This is what makes it critically important for men to have an outlet in which they can be vulnerable. In the previous section on *Fear of Insignificance* I mentioned a good friend with whom I have coffee weekly. This is where we can both be vulnerable with each other in a relationship of trust and confidentiality. I am blessed to have one or two other close friends who I can rely on for confidentiality and encouragement in my vulnerable times. It seems logical, if you're married or in a partnership, your significant other would be a likely point of refuge for sharing the things stored deep within your heart. It might seem logical, but it might not be practical. We want our loved ones to see us as strong and secure because we want them to feel safe and stable in a relationship with us. There can be hesitation to share with our spouse/partner the hidden things that might have potential to cause them fear or pain. If we reveal the truth of our struggle with career, mental health, addiction, physical ailment, infidelity, or any other condition, there can be a fear our "house of cards" may collapse. Vulnerability can reveal our own sensitivity and fragility. If you fear this collapse, let me suggest vulnerability can also reveal your strength. In his letter to the church of Corinth, the apostle Paul wrote:

> " ... Therefore I will boast all the more gladly about my weaknesses, so that Christ's power may rest on me. That is why, for Christ's sake, I delight in weaknesses, in insults, in

hardships, in persecutions, in difficulties. For when I am weak, then I am strong." – 2 Corinthians 12: 9-10 (NIV)

Whether or not you are a Christian, this statement can be applied to you. In fact, many Christians interpret this statement incorrectly, believing they lack internal strength and must rely on an external-ized strength. This scripture is a reminder of the strength within us. It means when we feel emptied of our own strength, there is a reserve living within us. For the Christian, this reserve is the Holy Spirit – the Christ – the untapped strength. In his book, *The Universal Christ*, Richard Rohr offers an interesting perspective on "Christ" as being a form of spirituality or energy contained in all of creation – including each of us. He identifies our connectedness and relationship to others and to God as the factors allowing us to tap into our inner Christ.

Thought of in this context, it is through relationship and connect-edness we are made strong even in our moments of weakness. We've been created for connection. Connection strengthens us and helps us overcome the weakness we might experience when we're alone, iso-lated, or trying to conquer problems on our own. When connected we are strong and our vulnerability becomes a strength not only for us, but for others. This is why meetings of Alcoholics Anonymous are crucial to achieving and maintaining sobriety and reclaiming quality of life. The 12 steps reviewed in every AA meeting walk through a process of recognizing powerlessness, acknowledging a Higher Power, and focusing on connection through several paths. Each alcoholic has a sponsor to support them in their journey and a consistent group with whom they can share and who also benefit by sharing with each other. Vulnerability reveals strength when we come to recognize we are not alone. The thing we were afraid of no longer holds us captive. There is strength in freedom and vulnerability allows us to be free of whatever previously imprisoned us. If you consider vulnerability to be a weakness, I urge you to find a trusted friend, loved one, group, or mental health professional with whom you can become strong through vulnerability.

Fear of Disrespect

Respect is one of the greatest needs of all men. If we have the choice of being liked or being respected, we overwhelmingly choose respect. Respect from others is what provides us with a sense of dignity, worth, acceptance, and self-respect. This is evident in many of the couples I see in counseling. A man in a relationship who does not feel respected by his spouse/partner both feels and appears defeated. Many of the men I see (both in couple therapy and individually) have experienced the father wound of being disrespected through either verbal or physical abuse throughout childhood, adolescence and, for some, adulthood. For men, there is nothing more emasculating than to be treated with disrespect. In the face of disrespect we generally respond in one of two ways: withdraw or attack. Neither of which is healthy.

To withdraw in the face of disrespect sends a message of acceptance and invites more of it. In children this can be seen when a child is repeatedly bullied and experiences a form of learned helplessness – the belief there is nothing they can do to change their circumstance. They believe they have no choice other than to accept and experience the pain. In extreme cases this can lead to suicidal or homicidal actions.

To attack in the face of disrespect is to fight fire with fire, which in human relationships only serves to escalate conditions, potentially to the point of violence. Sometimes this "return fire" isn't directed toward the initial violator but instead causes the victim to turn their "gun" of disrespect toward someone else. The victim becomes the perpetrator or, in the example of childhood bullying, the bullied becomes the bully.

If you think I'm giving more attention to disrespect than it really deserves, think about the real guns young men have turned on other students in school shootings. Many of these young men have been disrespected to the point of desperation and vengeance. They are driven to withdrawal, but in withdrawal are planning their attack.

Is there a healthy response to disrespect? You bet.

Address it head on and be assertive, not violent. Let the person know the manner in which they're addressing you is unacceptable. Tell them it needs to stop and not be repeated. Let them know they're to address you respectfully and speak about you to others respectfully. Let them know, if they can't agree to this, either the relationship will be over or, in the case of school or work, their behavior will be reported. You deserve dignity and respect. Likewise, others deserve it from you.

Fear of Failure

Failure.

The word alone strikes fear in the heart of most men ... and boys. This is largely because, from childhood, we're conditioned to believe not getting expected results equals failure. If something doesn't turn out as well as we thought it would, it's a "failed plan." If a student does not meet a minimum expected grade, the student has "failed." I'd like to suggest we re-frame the entire concept of failure. Let's begin by being honest – all of us have experienced failure. Let's also be clear – experiencing failure does not make you a failure.

When something doesn't work out as we had hoped, such as a relationship, a job, a competition, a class, etc., we need to view it as a learning experience and not as a final result. "Failure" feels so final. Instead of viewing them as failures, I like to think of these learning experiences as being the next step toward success. I won't make light of the fact these learning experiences can sometimes be very painful and, perhaps, embarrassing. For example, to simply chalk up the end of a thirty-year relationship as a learning experience would be minimizing a nearly lifelong investment, whether it be to a marriage or career. The unexpected end of your life's work can be emotionally devastating and strike deeply at your sense of self. It can change more than just the direct relationship with your partner or job. It can change the connections you had with other people. It can change your financial stability. It can change the way you look at yourself.

When something doesn't work out as we expected, looking at ourselves is the first thing we should do. If we truly want to learn from the experience and move forward in a productive manner, we've got to take an honest look in the mirror and ask ourselves the following questions:

What were my expectations and what were the expectations of other(s)?

If we enter into an experience without any expectations, then we should expect nothing out of it. I think it's safe to say this applies to every experience, be it coffee with a friend or entering into a marriage or partnership. How we estimate expectations of a coffee meeting vs. a marriage/partnership will obviously be far different, but sometimes we underestimate what will be expected of an experience due to lack of understanding, lack of information, or being out of touch with reality (fantasizing). Here are some suggestions to consider in answering the question of expectations in the examples of marriage/partnership and work:

In marriage/partnership: What need are you trying to fulfill in entering the relationship? What attracts you to this person? How long have you known this person? How much do you really know about this person *and their family* (you are marrying both!)? Are you going to couples counseling? This last one is BIG! Here is why ... when we're dating or in the "honeymoon" stage of our relationship, we want to put our best foot forward and be what our partner wants us to be. It's very difficult to see beyond the veneer of our behaviors and expressed desires at this stage. This often requires a third party willing to ask the hard questions we fear asking of each other. Here are some questions a counselor might raise:

- What do you consider each of your roles in this relationship to be?

- Does each of you plan to either work or stay home? For how long?

- What is your approach to work: whatever it takes, 40 hours per week, or something in between?

- How much time do you like to spend socializing with others individually and as a couple?

- What do you expect to do together and separately?

- What does each of you desire out of your sexual relationship?

- Do you want children? If so, how many? When?

- What are your spiritual beliefs and practices?

- If you have children, what spiritual environment do you want them raised in?

- What are you willing to sacrifice for each other?

- Do you want to rent or own?

- How much debt are you bringing into the relationship?

- How do you define financial success?

- How do you feel about having a budget?

- How do you feel about financial investment? In what? Starting when?

- Is there anything you have avoided telling your partner up to this point in your relationship?

… and this is just scratching the surface.

In work: What is required of the position? Does this align with your competencies and values? What are your employer's expectations of you? What are your expectations of your employer? How do you define success in this employment relationship? What is the culture of the company? What is the reputation of this company and its leadership? What is the financial strength of this company? What are your opportunities for advancement within this company? What are your desires for advancement? What are the company's desires/needs for your advancement? What criteria are in place for determining advancement?

If these and other questions have not been asked, expectations of everyone involved may not be understood. If you're reading this and you haven't yet been in a relationship or work experience, I strongly encourage you to do the work of answering these questions with the people you are involved with before making a long-term commitment. You might just save yourself a lot of pain and heartache.

Were my expectations and their expectations reasonable?

If you asked no questions or very few questions, your expectations may not have been reasonable. When expectations are not communicated, it can be assumed they will not be understood. Unspoken expectations will, most often, not be met and can lead to disappointment. Let's look at an example of a college student whose parents have pushed their child toward medical school even though their child's sole desire has always been to be an artist. If the expectations of both the parents and the child are not communicated and discussed with an open mind before choosing the education and career path, mutual expectations may not be met. Agreement on reasonable expectations is required from the start if reasonable results are to be expected. Keep in mind, however, desires and expectations can change over time. In the examples used above for expectations of marriage and work, if a thorough job of asking about and communicating expectations was done and the expectations seemed reasonable at the time, something may have changed in either your desires or the desires of others.

What changed and what was my role in the change?

It's important to realize change is constant and the work done entering into an experience needs to continue to be done. If we don't recognize this, we can be caught flat-footed by change either as it happens or after it happens. This can result in some of the most difficult learning of all. We've got to take an honest look at how we changed or identify how we missed change happening around us. If we are to experience growth from change and not allow ourselves to be unexpectedly affected by it, we have to invest time for discussion with others involved. This might mean we have to acknowledge our complacency in meeting the expectations of others or we need to forgive those who failed to communicate new conditions or expectations to us. The question then is…

How do I respond to unmet expectations?

First, acknowledge you are human - we all make mistakes, we all mess up, and we all feel like we should have done something to prevent it. Second, don't allow your mistakes or the things that happen to you to define you. Third, recognize the only thing you can control is you, including how you respond. Here are my suggestions:

- Give yourself some time to recover from the experience.

- Allow yourself to grieve if necessary (failure can be experienced as loss).

- If helpful to you, find a friend, a group, or a professional to help you process your experience.

- Reconnect with people who are supportive and encouraging.

- Having learned, grown, and forgiven (either yourself or others) … start again.

- Affirm yourself in your journey and your next step in moving forward.

- Start over again, and begin by asking yourself and others the questions:
    - What are my expectations and what are the expectations of other(s)?
    - Are my expectations and their expectations reasonable?

The bottom line to fear of failure is this - it can paralyze you. But it doesn't need to and it shouldn't. We will all experience mistakes and disappointment at some point in our life simply because we are not in control of all events. Even when we feel we're in control, mistakes leading to unmet expectations will happen. This doesn't make you a failure, it makes you human. Don't be afraid! Prepare in the best way you can and seek the help of others when going into new experiences. Go in with as many questions answered as possible and then seize the day! It's an old basketball adage, but it is the absolute truth – "You miss 100% of the shots you don't take." Prepare well and take the shot!

Think of your life as a journey. On this journey you will have many opportunities to enjoy views, stop at landmarks, meet people, and visit friends. Ultimately we'll all complete our journey. As we look back, we'll remember and cherish all of the great experiences. In the midst of these experiences we may have been taken off our planned course due to unexpected traffic, road construction, or detours. We may have missed an exit and circled back or found a different exit to get us to the same place. The point is this: consider failing as one more opportunity to succeed. Failure is nothing more than a detour or a missed exit. Our journey continues with new insight, new views and, sometimes, new people. If you're frustrated with the journey, exit at a rest stop and take time to consider what it will take for you to move forward and enjoy the rest of your trip. Then get back on the road and keep going. Failure is not the ending, it's a new beginning.

Now ... back to the original question: What are you afraid of?

Have you identified with any of the above fears based on your past or present circumstances? Have you conditioned yourself to respond to certain fear-producing situations or circumstances in an unhealthy manner?

We all have fears and some of them are hard to separate and identify. For example, disrespect can lead to feelings of rejection. Rejection can cause feelings of insignificance. Insignificance can result in feelings of loss. All of these feelings and fears can make us feel extremely vulnerable because we judge ourselves as "not good enough" or "failures." We can become our own worst critic and become paralyzed by fear of judgment if we're not careful.

I'd like you to think about what provokes fear in you and share your fear with a trusted friend, partner, or professional. Consider where, when, or how the fear originated. Consider whether it is rational or beneficial to you. Some fears are healthy and justified, but most are not. Don't be held captive by fears or let them steal your joy and quality of life. We weren't created to be slaves to fear. Take heart and remember courage is not the absence of fear, but the overcoming of fear.

Summary Points of FEAR

- You don't have to be perfect to be good.

- Let fear motivate you, not paralyze you.

- Ask yourself: What past event causes you fear? Is it rational?

- Your life is essential. Your impact is significant.

- Vulnerability reveals strength when we come to recognize we are not alone.

- Demand respect and give respect.

- Experiencing failure does not make you a failure.

- Expectations should be identified and made known in advance.

- Recognize and address modified expectations.

- Failure is not an ending, it's a new beginning.

- Courage is not the absence of fear, but the overcoming of fear.

- Talk to a trusted friend or counselor about your fears.

- "… often it is such a difficult external situation which gives man opportunity to grow spiritually beyond himself." - Viktor Frankl, Holocaust survivor.

Questions for Reflection

- What do you fear?

- How does it feel to be viewed by others as "average" at something important to you?

- How have you felt rejection in your life and how has it affected you, either positively or negatively?

- When in your life have you felt insignificant? If you were able to move beyond this feeling, how did you do so? If not, who can help you?

- How has the fear of vulnerability affected you? Who else has been affected by your ability or inability to be vulnerable?

- How have you experienced and responded to disrespect in the past?

- What failure have you experienced and how has it affected you? Have you moved beyond it? If so, how?

- Can you recall a time when fear transitioned to courage? If so, what impact did it have on your life?

- If you had a "do-over," how would you change the effect of fear on your life? What is necessary on your part to get a "do-over," starting today?

7

SUCCESS AND CONTENTMENT

I've heard it said the guy who dies with the most toys wins. Ironically, I don't know of anyone who has ever been able to prove this theory. After all ... who are we going to ask?

Our desire for "more" goes all the way back to the beginning of humanity. Whether you believe in the theory of evolution or intelligent design, humanity has always desired more. In the case of evolution, more was needed for survival of the fittest. The one who was bigger, stronger, and faster would thrive. The one who had more food, had secure shelter, and had more tools for survival would be the one able to proliferate and sustain survival of the species. In the case of intelligent design theory (in the context of the creation story provided in the Bible), the "more" was identified by the Tree of Knowledge. Eating from it was to gain knowledge and be like God. Knowledge equaled power, and humans wanted to have the power of God. The one with the most power survives. Whichever theory you subscribe to, I think we can all agree we've wanted more than we have for a long, long time. This desire for more has moved beyond the need for mere survival and, today, has become more about comfort and luxuries.

In Chapter 1, EXPLORING VALUES, I talked about priorities. How we define success in our own lives depends upon our values and priorities. While it's easy to leap to the conclusion that a desire for "more" represents a misguided definition of success, it really comes down to the motivation of our heart. If I want more money and my motives for this gain are altruistic, i.e. helping the poor … then having more money for helping others would be a true means of achieving success. The success would not be in the measurement of money obtained, but in the measurement of help provided to the poor. Likewise, if I acquire material possessions useful to meeting the needs of others, this is a good thing. There is nothing wrong with wealth and riches. Many will argue against this, saying, "Money is the root of all evil." This is often misquoted from scripture which actually says, "The love of money is the root of all evil." What's the difference? Motivation.

We all have selfish desires influencing our definition of success. My belief is, if we are growing and maturing in a healthy manner, our definition can change. When I graduated from college, I wanted to join a construction company that built big buildings all over the country and then start my own company to create great wealth for myself. As I learned the industry and its complexities, I recognized the level of problems and stress involved in ownership was not conducive to my desire for happiness. This was not a cost I was willing to pay. As a result, I re-evaluated how I could be successful. I realized I could be happier growing within the company and achieving higher levels of responsibility and higher pay. Along the way I had a tendency to compare myself to my peers - where they were in their advancement and the luxuries they were able to afford. I was where I wanted to be but I was still unhappy as I compared their "stuff" to mine. Some had speed boats, others took exotic vacations, and others drove big expensive trucks. I didn't have this kind of stuff because I couldn't afford it. The reason I couldn't afford it was not because I wasn't making enough, but because Denise was giving it away. She saw giving to the church and the community as an important responsibility of ours. I didn't. I looked at how much I was making, what stuff I could have bought and compared what I had to what others had. As a result, I was unhappy –

even in my wealth. My definition of success was about material wealth for my own comfort and luxury and making sure, compared to my peers, I made it to the grave with more than they had.

A pastor once told me comparison is the enemy of contentment (actually, he preached this message in a sermon, but I'm pretty sure he was speaking directly to me). There are many examples of guys who, like me, measured themselves against others and found no satisfaction in what they had acquired. There is story after story of professional athletes and celebrities who had enough money to buy anything they wanted - and did. But "more" was never enough. Some would continue to buy more stuff. Some would find a new relationship. Some would look for the next, better high. None of it was ever enough. As I matured in age, experience and faith, I came to learn if we define success by what we attain for ourselves without thought of what we can do for others, we come up short every time. Denise led me to the understanding and belief that there is not only a responsibility to provide for the needs of others, but there is joy in doing so. Over the years (many years) I came to the realization that if I could give to others and find contentment in my faith, family, work, and friendships, then I would have been successful. I stopped comparing myself to others and measured my success by what was important to me. In my life I have found contentment and joy in the blessings of a beautiful wife, caring children, unimaginably perfect grandchildren, and good friends.

My definition of success is not meant to cast judgment on anyone else's definition. Ultimately, success is about achieving what we want. Some are clear, committed and driven to achieve their version of success and live very happy, healthy and successful lives in which they are content. Others are clear, committed and driven but recognize, at some point, what they thought would define success for them, in fact, didn't. Changing course to re-define your version of success is not failure, it is being honest with yourself regarding what will bring you contentment and moving in a new direction to achieve it. Success cannot be defined by society for any of us because success is unique to each of us. Some wish to remain single. Some wish to marry but not have children. Some wish not to marry but to have children. Success can only be individually defined. If you're not content, you need to continue on your path toward success and understand a dead end only indicates the need for new direction.

Summary Points of SUCCESS AND CONTENTMENT

- Success and contentment is not necessarily defined by wealth.

- Motivation for gaining wealth can be for personal gain or for giving to others.

- Comparison is the enemy of contentment.

- Success is about achieving what we want, based upon our values.

- Success is unique to each of us.

Questions for Reflection

- Based upon your current values and priorities, how do you define success?

- How has your definition of success changed over your lifetime?

- Do you compare yourself to others? If so, in what areas of life?

- What, if anything, do you need to add or subtract from your life to consider yourself successful and content?

8

LEADING AND INFLUENCING

No matter how old you are, you can think back on your life and identify those who have modeled leadership to you. It may have been a parent, a sibling, a teacher, a coach, a friend, a pastor, a business associate, a boss, or others. Whoever it may be, there is at least one person in each of our lives who led us well enough for us to want to model ourselves after them. Sometimes it was not an individual, but a collection of individuals with different styles and gifts for leadership. Likewise, we've each probably had a leader in our life who was useful for only one thing – a bad example. This is the person (I use the singular form because I hope you haven't had more than one) from whom we learn the equally important lesson of who we don't want to be and how we don't want to act. The purpose in studying the leadership style of others is to adopt for ourselves a style of leadership which we consider to be highly effective. Effective leaders influence the next generation of leaders.

When you recognize the leaders in your life, you recognize their influence on your life. Leaders model thoughts and behaviors for us. Generally when we think of great leaders in history, we think about positive examples such as Abraham Lincoln. But there are also negative examples of great leaders, such as Adolf Hitler. My identification of Adolf Hitler as a great leader may offend you. My intent is not to identify him as "good person," but as a leader who effectively built an empire, communicated a message, and led a movement – albeit seriously misguided. There is no question he had great evil in him. Thank God his empire crumbled and his influence on the world was squelched - tragically, not soon enough and not completely enough. All leaders can have great influence. It can be either good or bad. Who are you leading and how are you influencing them?

While all leaders are influencers, not all influencers are leaders. Imagine hiking with twenty other people up a mountain trail, single file. You're in the middle of the line. Everyone is following the leader, who knows the trail and the destination. He's walking so fast that, while many can keep up, the last person in the line cannot. Multiple breaks are required to allow the last person to catch up. The last person is not leading, but he or she is certainly influencing the group. I imagine we can all come up with many ways in which a bad leader would handle this. Since my desire is to have a positive influence on you so you can have a positive influence on others, my focus will be on what good leadership looks like. After all, you are a leader whether you realize it or not. There is someone observing you. They pay attention to how you conduct yourself and how you treat others as you navigate life. They look at how you make decisions and strive to achieve goals. It may be a child, a spouse, a friend, or a business associate, but someone is watching. This person or these people will follow your lead. Here are several things to consider as you lead them:

Show Respect – Remember the Golden Rule. Everyone deserves respect. Showing it is a way of honoring someone's importance and acknowledging their significance.

Exercise Humility – Exercising humility is not thinking less of yourself, rather it is thinking less about yourself and more about others. It is a willingness to think in terms of what is best for others and what is best for everyone instead of what is best for me. Humility means not thinking of ourselves as being above others and not lording our position over anyone.

Be a Servant – Servant leadership is, in my opinion, the most effective leadership style. It communicates to those following you your willingness to do whatever it takes for the good of the entire team. In the example of the group hiking the mountain trail it could mean the leader is willing to carry the backpack of the last one in the line who is struggling to keep up. It is about a willingness to help and strengthen others.

Provide Guidance – A leader has to have a plan and know where they are leading the people who follow them. If someone is going to guide others, then they must have a guide of their own – a help on their own journey. A leader needs a compass to be a compass for others.

Have Goals – Guidance without goals is called "being lost." Short-term and long-term goals are important for every organization and every person. Without them we are aimless in the things we do and will lack structure in the process of making decisions. Every decision made should feed into the achievement of an overall goal. If we're presented with the opportunity to act on an option that will not earnestly help us move toward one of our goals, the decision on that option should be "no."

Ask Questions – A leader is not expected to know everything, but is expected to know how to ask questions … not just any questions – the right questions. This means if an answer or a process is not understood, we need to be humble enough to admit we don't "get it" and keep asking questions until we do. We also have to make it safe for others to ask questions of us. A sarcastic or a mocking response toward someone who is trying to understand what we're doing will immediately cut off open communication.

Get the Right People – If we want the right answers, we need to surround ourselves with the right people. For good leadership, we need to surround ourselves with people who are smarter than we are – those whose expertise goes beyond our own.

Listen Openly – There is great wisdom in keeping our mouths shut and our minds open. I mentioned a moment ago how sarcasm and mockery will shut down communication – as will disregarding requested input. This is not to say all input must be followed, but all input must be given consideration and receive thoughtful responses.

Have Fun! – Who wants to follow a sourpuss? Herb Kelleher, who co-founded and later led Southwest Airlines for twenty years, was known for his outrageous and fun-loving personality, which became the hallmark of the company culture. People wanted to work for Herb and fly Southwest Airlines "for peanuts" because of the culture of fun and humor the company embraced. They also happened to have a killer operational model keeping them profitable year after year while the airlines trying to prevent their start-up operated in the red. Herb and Southwest Airlines literally got the last laugh!

Be Positive – You have to believe in yourself and in those around you and communicate your confidence in their abilities. If you're an athlete, you understand the importance of this and how a good coach can make all of the difference by simply pushing and encouraging you. You get to the point where you have nothing left to give. You're out of breath. Your heart is pounding. You need to stop or you'll collapse. Then you hear your coach and your teammates: *"Push!!! ... Let's go!!! ... You can do this!!! ... C'mon, man!!!"* You find an energy reserve allowing you to go beyond what you thought you were capable of. Positivity is a powerful motivator.

Be Honest – Tell the truth – even when it hurts. Honesty without risk is easy. Honesty that could cost you a job, a relationship, or an opportunity is not. Leaders must learn to be candid with people. However, being honest gives no one permission to be brutal. Honesty can and should be delivered with candor and sensitivity. Being honest also means we are honest about our own mistakes and accept accountability for our errors.

Show Integrity – What do you do when no one is watching? What do you do if you know you won't get caught? These are both questions of integrity. Integrity goes beyond honesty vs. dishonesty. It goes beyond whether something is legal or illegal. Integrity has to do with morality vs. immorality and what is ethical vs. unethical. Integrity indicates an assurance of what someone can expect from you under any circumstances, good or bad.

Communicate the Message – A leader who has all of the other positive traits of leadership but is unable to clearly communicate his or her message will not be an effective leader and will frustrate followers. The clarity and accuracy of the message is critical whether it is communicated verbally, in writing, or in action. Business associates will, most likely, expect your communications to be in all three realms. Children will receive the message based on the behavior you model. Choose carefully the message you wish to communicate and then do so clearly.

Provide Inspiration – We choose to follow those who share our values and represent them in an admirable way. These leaders inspire us toward aspirational achievements through their own actions which go above and beyond the established standards. Inspirational leadership is focused on achievement, justice, and the general welfare.

Be Courageous – Have you ever heard the phrase "God hates a coward"? I'm actually not a big fan of it, but if you're of the John Wayne mentality or find yourself occasionally shouting "*Oorah!*" it might be helpful to you. For the rest of us more mild-mannered types, let's look at courage not as the absence of fear but as the ability to work through it. Followers are reassured by leaders who provide a calm, quiet, measured, and confident response in the face of adversity. If you consider it cowardly not to run immediately into battle when challenged, reconsider. Consider, instead, demonstrating courage by overcoming impulsivity with a measured and thoughtful response.

Encourage Creativity – Thinking "outside of the box" and promoting this habit among your followers encourages them to get out of the "that's the way we've always done it" mentality, which only generates the same results you've always had. Creative thinking, modeled by you, empowers those who follow you to do the same and come up with new and better ways of getting things done.

Value Relationships – I was twenty-four years old when my father died. He was sick for a couple of years prior to his death, so I didn't really have the opportunity, once I had entered the business world, to learn much from him about how to be successful in that environment. If he had lived longer, I'm certain he would have told me to value relationships and treat people well. Don't get me wrong, my father taught me as a child to be a good person and to care for others. I did this growing up and I tried to be a good person in my personal life as a young adult, but I thought the business world was different – more cutthroat. I needed to learn to value relationships in business because, being young and competitive, I believed there can only be one winner. I'm embarrassed to say I was probably eighteen years into my career before a man I had just started working for, James Turner, came into my office and said, "Chris, I want you to think more about your relationships with people. The success of our business depends on how much we value the relationships with the people we buy from and sell to." He literally spoke to me as a father and I will be forever grateful for the gentle correction he provided me early on in my tenure with him. It changed my attitude and had a great impact on how I approached business from that day forward. It's not about me, it's about us. I'm sure my father would thank James for giving me the advice and give me a wink and a pat on the back for following it.

Have Vision – In the realm of business, vision can mean focusing on meeting one quarterly goal at a time or focusing on the goals for the company five to ten years from now. Both are important. It's really not an either/or choice. The ability to focus on the short term and have a well communicated vision for the future are both critical to the team. Vision should motivate and generate excitement. Vision should be ambitious. Vision should include what Jim Collins, in his book *Built to Last,* refers to as "BHAGS" (Big Hairy Audacious Goals). In your visioning process, dream beyond what you've always imagined.

Do the same for those who follow you in your personal life. Wouldn't you want to dream big and have a vision for your children as well? This doesn't mean you're going to choose their college or career for them, but you are going to try to help them develop the character traits necessary to achieve their own dreams. What vision do you have for your children and what can you teach them now with that vision in mind? A good starting point would be the list you're reading from right now. After all, good leaders, who positively influence others, must first learn to be good people.

Admittedly, this is a long list of leadership traits. I'm in big trouble if having all of them is a prerequisite for effective leadership. In fact, there's only one guy I've ever heard of who mastered all of them. He was a homeless Jewish carpenter who was killed a little over 2,000 years ago because the establishment of the time didn't like the message he was communicating. But he had a rag-tag group of twelve guys who hung out with him. They bought into his message and told a few others about it. Today he has about 2.4 billion followers worldwide ... now that's effective leadership! Granted, we're not all going to be quite as effective in delivering a message and developing a following as Jesus, but we can use the skills we've been given. We can listen to advice and learn from others. We can identify what doesn't work well. We can surround ourselves with good, intelligent people. We can make a plan. We can be honorable and respectful. We can show appreciation and be bold. We can make it a point to have some fun. Sounds more reasonable than being an expert in all areas, doesn't it? Good. Have fun and lead on.

Summary points of LEADING AND INFLUENCING

- Model your leadership style after the highly effective leaders in your life.
- You are a leader and influencer, whether you realize it or not.
- Lead well by:
  Showing respect
  Exercising humility
  Being a servant
  Providing guidance
  Having goals
  Asking questions
  Surrounding yourself with the right people
  Listening openly
  Having fun!
  Being positive
  Being honest
  Showing integrity
  Communicating clearly
  Providing inspiration
  Being courageous
  Encouraging creativity
  Valuing relationships
  Having vision

Questions for Reflection

- Who were/are the effective leaders in your life? What made/makes them memorable and effective?

- Of the leadership traits listed in this chapter, which of them are most highly developed in you? Who can you help in development of these traits?

- Of the leadership traits listed in this chapter, which of them would you most like to focus on for further development? Who do you consider to be a strong leader in these areas and available to help you?

- Who are the experts you surround yourself with in your leadership as a husband, father, or co-worker?

9

TRANSITIONS

My family has always been close and very well connected. Denise and I enjoyed activities with our girls from the time they were too young to remember. We loved the outdoors – sightseeing, hiking, skiing, and all types of youth sports. We traveled a lot together on weekends, especially when both of the girls were in competitive swimming. They both excelled in it and both stayed involved in water sports through their college years. Stephanie, our oldest, was the first to leave the nest. I remember the excitement in our discussions about college and taking college visits with her. Living in the Dallas area, there were plenty of great colleges in the immediate area and even more within a few hours of home. Swim coaches from Texas Christian University (TCU), The University of North Texas (UNT) and Texas A&M University expressed interest in her joining their programs. I was excited about the prospect of having her relatively close to home and being able to attend most, if not all, of her college swim meets.

She had other ideas. She had always dreamed of swimming at Texas A&M University, but the best they could offer her was a position as a walk-on (non-scholarship). She eventually determined she wasn't interested in a walk-on role because she would not get to compete in "away" meets. She knew the work it required and decided, if she was going to swim, she was going to swim in all meets and compete. I admired her desire to compete because this was a very tough decision for her to make. She also immediately ruled out TCU and UNT because they were too close to home and she felt the need to "cut the cord." She said, "If I go to either of those schools, you and Mom will want me to come home every weekend." Someday she will have children in high school. They will tell her how unreasonable, unfair, uncool, non-understanding, and impossible she is. In that moment she will understand the absolute fallacy in believing we would want her home from college every weekend.

She knew she had other options because she had received invitations to visit several schools, one of which was the University of Arkansas. She was excited about this opportunity and, even though it was six hours from home, so was I.

The sports programs at Arkansas are very strong, the campus is beautiful, and the academics are top-notch. She decided to accept this offer to visit, so we all loaded up the car and went to see the university and meet the coach. The visit was a great success. The facilities for women's sports programs were second to none, and the academic staff was phenomenal in the time they spent with her and the interest they showed in her. By the way, this is not simply because she was an athlete. I have heard the same experience from every other parent who has taken a son or daughter to visit the university … way to go, Arkansas! Based on our visit, I knew Stephanie's decision to go to Arkansas was a slam dunk and I couldn't have been more proud of my daughter being a Razorback swimmer! There was one more visit we would make out of courtesy to a very nice coach at a school in Missouri. It was six hours farther north from Fayetteville. I kept my thoughts to myself about canceling the second leg of the trip because Stephanie told the coach she would visit, so we did. The school was nice, but it was twelve hours away from home and in the backwoods of northeast Missouri.

On the long, long, long ... long drive home from Missouri, I could sense the excitement in the car. About two weeks later, as I was sitting in my recliner watching television one evening, Stephanie came out of her room beaming with pride and told me she had just spoken to the coach and accepted a scholarship offer! The moment had arrived! I was overjoyed and so was she as she continued to tell me how impressed she had been with the coach and how much she loved visiting with the swimmers at Truman State University!

Wait ... what?

It took all of my strength to muster the words, "That's great, Stephanie!" Never have such false words been uttered by any father in the history of mankind. I was stunned. It wasn't that I had anything against Truman State University. Wait ... yes I did. *It was twelve hours away!*

I was excited about Stephanie's transition to college, but thought she would be closer to home. I wasn't ready for this amount of separation from her and it hit me like a ton of bricks. Since I spoke about vulnerability in the previous chapter, I'll stay true to it ... I couldn't sleep that night. I was sitting alone at the kitchen table, crying, at about 1:00 in the morning. She hadn't left yet and I already missed her. I was angry with God for taking her so far from me. A little selfish, yes ... but I'm a guy.

Transitions we aren't prepared for can be tough, even if we knew the transition was coming. Being aware of a transition and being prepared for the transition are two entirely different things. Being entirely unaware of a transition is a real blindside. It catches you completely flat-footed.

Being caught completely unaware by change can happen when focus is on the wrong thing, complacency sets in, or when someone trusted simply acts with deceit. Many have experienced a sudden and stunning job loss. Perhaps they were unaware of changing conditions in the corporate winds or perhaps they became comfortable and less focused on expectations of them. This can also happen in relationships. Maybe you know someone whose spouse/partner ended the re-lationship, taking them by complete surprise. Difficult transitions can include a wide range of feelings, including both sadness and anger. The important thing to remember about any difficult transition is it's just that ... a transition. Life goes on, perhaps differently - even if it involves significant and difficult loss.

Although transition may represent the end of one thing, it can also be viewed as the start of another. Transition is not an end in and of itself. How we view transition is largely dependent upon how resilient we are to change. In Chapter 3, CONTROL, I said we choose the way we think. When difficult changes in our life take us by surprise we have a choice to make. One option is to live in the pain of it and allow ourselves to adopt the new identity of "victim." The other option is to move forward with a commitment to live life to its fullest. Many are even able to move into an improved life. It's important for me to point this out: I'm not insensitive to the pain, grief, and suffering of those whose transition involves the loss of a loved one. I would not dare imply there is not a lifelong impact or there is a way to simply "move forward." I know better. That would be completely irresponsible and, in my mind, reprehensible. With any negative transition there is grief and pain, the depth and duration of which will vary depending upon the degree of the sense of loss. What I want to convey here is reason for hope once we have been able to lift our heads and look forward once again.

We saw an example of the possibilities for making a successful transition in Chapter 6, FEAR. This was the story of my friend whose position was suddenly classified as "non-essential." His transition was unexpected, yet he accomplished it decisively and effectively. He is now living into his true calling as a professional counselor. In my own story of having my oldest daughter leave the nest, I was able to tran-sition to a positive mindset. It was a mindset celebrating Stephanie's joy and excitement as she transitioned into collegiate swimming and a new environment. If I may exercise a father's pride for a moment, please allow me to tell the rest of the story regarding her time at Truman State University ... as if you have a choice. Stephanie quickly befriended the other swimmers on the team. She even fell in love with one of them and married him in Dallas in 2009. Nearly every one of their former teammates flew in from Nebraska, Iowa, Illinois, and Missouri to attend. Ten years later we're blessed to say not only do Stephanie and Alex live fifteen minutes from us, but (better yet) so do the two beautiful grandchildren they've given us! One more thing ... the Truman State University Women's Swim Team won the Division 2A National Championship three out of the four years Stephanie was there. Who would have thought fifteen years ago I'd be saying this today: GO BULLDOGS!!!

Summary Points of TRANSITIONS

- Anticipate and prepare, to the best of your ability, for the transitions you know will come.

- Even if loss is experienced, transition is not an end in and of itself.

- You have a choice in your response to transition.

- Even in the transitions involving loss and grief, over time a sense of peace can emerge.

- Transitions can result in great things!

Questions for Reflection

- What known transitions will occur in your life? How much have you thought about them and how well are you prepared for them?

- What unexpected transitions have occurred in your life? How difficult was it to deal with these changes?

- Even in a transition involving loss, were you able over time to see the beginning of something new ... something that, were it not for your loss, may not have been experienced or recognized?

10

IDENTITY

What is your essence?

I'm hoping you haven't just walked into a bookstore, picked this book off the shelf, opened it randomly to this page and read that sentence. If so, thanks for your interest ... you can find *Wild at Heart* by John Eldredge on the New York Times Bestseller rack at the store entrance.

If you've decided to continue reading, indulge me for a moment while I put this question in context. My dictionary app provides this definition for "essence":

"The basic, real, and invariable nature of a thing or its significant individual feature or features"

In other words, our essence is who we are at our core. This includes what we think about, what we believe about ourselves and others, our worldview, and what is meaningful in life. It's interesting to think about how, essentially, we are all the same. All of our real and basic needs are invariable no matter our nationality, race, religion, culture, gender, age, or sexual orientation.

In 1943, a psychologist by the name of Abraham Maslow wrote a paper entitled "A Theory of Human Motivation." His paper proposed a five-tier model of human need which came to be known as Maslow's

Hierarchy of Needs. It is typically presented in the form of a pyramid. The base of the pyramid represents our most basic human physiological needs. The top of the pyramid represents our self-fulfillment needs. This hierarchy is shown below. It may be helpful to refer to this as we explore our essence, our self-image, the image we want others to see, and the image others actually see. If this sounds like a bunch of psycho-babble, let me put it another way: Looks can be deceiving.

Maslow's Hierarchy of Needs

- Level 1 represents the basic physiological needs shared by every human being – what it takes for individual and species survival.

- Level 2 also represents a basic need – the need to be safe and secure; not to feel endangered or threatened in our environment. In other words, the ability to live in peace and harmony with our environment.

- Level 3 moves us into representation of our psychological needs – the need for community, acceptance, and belonging.

- Level 4 represents fulfillment of another psychological need – the need for a sense of self-worth. Our self-worth is affected not only by how we think about and treat ourselves, but also by our perception of how others think about and treat us.

- Level 5, at the top of the pyramid, represents self-fulfillment – our self-actualized ability to pursue and do what brings joy, purpose and meaning to our lives.

Why is all of this important? Because if we are not having needs met at all five levels, then our overall quality of life and, potentially, our mental and physical health are at risk.

Our Essence

In addition to the definition previously provided, I like to think of our essence as what we are created for. I strongly believe every person has a purpose. We have prenatal physiological needs for healthy development including food, sleep, and shelter to keep us safe and secure in our mother's womb. Believe it or not, we also have prenatal social needs as we respond to the sounds of our environment (voices, music, etc.) and begin to develop a sense of belonging. Through infancy and childhood we increase social development and learn more about social cues in our interactions. This is where relationships are developed (or fail to develop in the absence of healthy interaction) and our sense of self is established. This all happens within the first few years of life and sets the course for positive self-esteem, self-confidence, and self-actualization. Our sense of self dictates our ability to be in healthy relationship with others. Being in relationship is, I believe, a common purpose for which we are all created. Each of us needs to be in relationship with others. It's this collective common purpose of being in relationship – our connectedness - that reveals our individual purpose and how it will best be fulfilled.

The interesting thing about our essence is, for many of us, we go through the better part of our lives without recognizing what it is. Instead, our self-image is formed by what society and our culture tell us. As a result, the essence of who we are becomes buried deep within us. There seems to be a formula for living with which we're expected to comply: we're born, we grow, we start school, we fall in love with someone of the opposite sex, we graduate from school, we start work, we get married, we buy a home, we have children, we raise them, we retire, and we die. There it is. Before we get to the last item in this chronology, we generally have time to reflect on life. Upon this reflection, we are either content or discontent. I'd like to think there is more to life than this bleak chronology. I believe if we are living into our essence, and not simply into the template for living, we can reflect on the past with great joy as well as experience great joy in the present.

Reflected Image

As adults, we talk a lot about how adolescents are very self-centered and self-conscious. When I say this, it sounds critical of an entire generation, but nothing could be farther from the truth. Adolescence is a time in life when body chemistry and physiology are changing dramatically. What the teenager experiencing this wants most is to be accepted, to belong, not to stand out in the crowd, to be independent and not to be the center of any negative (or sometimes positive) attention. Ironically, it's this desire *for* independence and *not to be* the center of attention causing them to center 100% of their attention on themselves. All of this to be sure of one thing: they're *just like* everyone else and don't call attention to themselves. Wow! That's a real setup for discontentment! Does this really end in adolescence? Is this really something affecting girls only? C'mon, man! Let's be honest. When you get ready to leave the house, do you ever check yourself in the mirror? It's not just an adolescent thing. We want to see what other people will be looking at. Is the hair right (assuming you've still got it)? Are the clothes fashionable? Is the make-up right (yes - this is also now a guy thing)? Do I look too fat? Do I look too skinny? Is this how people will want to see me? Will I be accepted?

We want others to see us in the way we'll be acceptable to them. Think about first dates. We pull out all the stops to be sure we look "just right" for whatever the event or activity might be. We want to be accepted and make a good first impression. The reflected image we see in the mirror is the first impression we create for others and we want it to be good...no matter our age, race, or gender. But truthfully, the reflected image doesn't go very deep. It's only what is seen on the surface ... and looks can be deceiving. Sometimes the good-looking image in the mirror is nothing more than an empty shell. We can look great on the outside to others and be anything but great on the inside. This incongruity happens when we aren't being true to ourselves ... to the essence of who we are.

Self-image

We can generate either a positive or negative self-image, both of which depend upon how honest and true we're being with ourselves. When we're being one person on the outside and another person on the inside we live in a state of dysregulation, which creates stress and tension. We're either trying *to be* someone we are not or trying *not to be* someone who, in essence, we are. Examples of this might include being in an unfulfilling course of study or working in a career projected on us due to the expectations of others. It might be we're participating in things we don't enjoy because of peer pressure. It might be we're hiding an addiction others can't see. It could be we're not exposing a side of ourselves for fear of how others will respond. The more conflicted we are with ourselves the more likely we are to suffer from low self-esteem and other symptoms of depression.

Conversely, when we focus on our internal feelings and the passions we're naturally drawn to, we're less concerned about living into the expectations of others. We think about healthier things, believe in the goodness of ourselves and others, find purpose and meaning in what we do and our worldview is one of hope - not despair. We're not trying to follow a template designed by others and for others. As a result, we are able to experience peace and joy in life … what some refer to as "heaven on earth." Everything about us doesn't have to be perfect for this to occur. When we look in the mirror, every one of us looks past the beauty in how we're created and immediately finds the blemishes. I won't go into the detail of the blemishes I see in my mirror, but suffice it to say I'd be okay if my nose was a little more like Brad Pitt's, my smile was a little more like George Clooney's, and my cheek bones were a little more like Johnny Depp's. That said, I'm content with Chris Robinson. I look in the mirror and, despite not being perfect in appearance, I'm happy with who I am. I am content in the life I'm living and I don't worry at all about trying to look like or be like someone else. As the saying goes, "you be you" and people will appreciate you for your authenticity and genuineness despite your imperfections. Don't get caught up in who you want to look or be like … just tell me who you are.

Self-Identity

It's easy to ignore who we really are for the sake of who we want to be. In my young adulthood the thoughts guiding my actions revolved around being in a position of respect and influence with a company valuing hard work and loyalty. Following his military service, my father had been in a job like this in the petroleum industry. He was with one company for his entire career. My grandfather had done the same, working for the federal government. Ironically, the one field my father suggested I stay away from was the petroleum industry. Although he had been financially successful, it was apparent by his recommendation he was left unfulfilled by his career. At the time he gave me this advice I was too self-centered to inquire about his reasons for giving it. Now having more life experience, I recognize the reason he had a heart attack at age fifty-four and died from cancer at the age of fifty-eight had much to do with the stress involved in his work. He wanted better for me.

When I went to college, he was pleased with my decision to pursue a degree in something I loved. Four years later I graduated with my degree in Building Construction from Texas A&M University and went to work with J.W. Bateson Company in Dallas. This was a construction company with a great reputation doing work all over the country. I was proud to be part of this organization and to be associated with all of the dedicated people who worked there. I progressed well over the years and was promoted into an executive position. Bateson was the subsidiary of another large national corporation which, over the years, rebranded the company using different names. After several years they brought in a new president from outside the company in an effort to increase volume and profits. When a new president is brought in to run a company, often the first order of business is to replace existing management with people familiar to the new leader and supportive of his or her leadership style. I learned this the hard way. This meant that after seventeen years, I was relieved of my duties. More plainly put – fired. In one afternoon my world was turned upside down.

I always believed, like my father and grandfather, I would have a career with a company that honored commitment, hard work, and loyalty from its employees. I thought I would start and finish my career with the same organization. I took pride in being employed by this company and was proud of the work I did. The people there were more like family than co-workers. My self-identity was wrapped around my employment and success within this company. When I was fired everything about my self-identity crumbled to the ground like a pile of rubble. The last thing I want this story to be for you is a "woe is me" tale. Nothing could be farther from the truth. I grieved deeply over this loss and it took a long time for me to feel the same about myself as a professional in this industry. Eventually, however, I regained my confidence and began to enjoy success once again – but with a different understanding of my own identity.

Make no mistake, if you have suffered the indignity of being fired it's not something you would wish on your worst enemy. However, I now refer to this firing as the best thing that ever happened to me. It forced me to re-evaluate myself and my priorities. It set me upon a new trajectory which led me to the fulfillment I enjoy today. My own success, for all of my career up to the point of being fired, had been defined by my work. Work and professional success were the most important things in my life because they allowed me to afford the things I wanted to provide for my family.

I want you to read the last sentence again and pause before you go further. Think about the logic of it.

That is some warped thinking. If it's the logic you use in establishing your self-identity and your priorities, I want to ask you to do something ... stop it.

It didn't happen right away, but upon reflection I realized my core values were way out of whack (refer to Chapter 1, EXPLORING VALUES). I came to an understanding: my faith and family should be more important and more valuable to me than anything else. I learned spending time with my wife and children should take priority over the time spent at work. I needed to abandon self-seeking stature in my career. If I was to seek adoration it should be from my family and not from my co-workers or business associates. I learned my family cared more about my presence than our wealth. There is a very subtle but important difference in placing work as a priority to provide for family vs. placing family as a priority for which you work. Without being fired I might never have come to this understanding and would have been perfectly comfortable in the neglect of both faith and family for the purpose of professional success. Guys ... placement of work as the number one priority in our lives is part of the cultural and societal norm we are expected to accept. It is a completely warped sense of priorities for us to live into if we have a family depending upon us to be present as a husband and a father.

If you hear me saying professional success as a number one priority is wrong, let me clarify. There is nothing wrong with setting this as your number one priority if you are not in committed relationships where others depend upon you for emotional support. If you've explored your values and set your mind to make career success your number one priority, you've made a perfectly legitimate choice. That choice will require you to be fully present in your profession. The trap to avoid is fooling yourself into thinking there can be two number one priorities.

Your self-identity needs to be given a lot of thought and reflection based upon your values. Your self-identity shouldn't be based upon what other people see in you or desire to see in you. Nor should it be based upon how you want others to see you. Self-identity is not about image. Your self-identity should be based upon the truth and confidence with which you live into your values. It doesn't matter what other people think. Be true to yourself and your values and you will be far happier in life. Carl Jung, the Swiss psychiatrist, spoke of exploring the unconscious as letting go of the surface things and dropping into the deep and vibrant water of the true self. He believed only then are we able to be fully and authentically alive. Explore and know who you are at your very essence and you will find your true identity.

Summary Points of IDENTITY

- Our essence is who we are at our core and the purpose we are created for.

- Being in relationship is a common purpose for which we are all created.

- We all want to be accepted by others.

- What is important is our self-image, not what others see.

- The more conflicted we are with ourselves, the lower our self-esteem.

- When our internal and external identities are aligned, we find peace and contentment.

- Our self-identity should be based upon the truth and confidence with which we live into our values.

Questions for Reflection

- Throughout your life, how well do you think your needs were met when viewed through the lens of Maslow's Hierarchy? How might fulfillment (or lack thereof) of these needs shape your self-identity and behavior today?

- How would you define the essence of who you are?

- What purpose were you created for?

- How well do you find your essence and purpose respected and supported by those with whom you are in relationship?

- What reflected image are you trying to create? Does this desired external image conflict with the essence of who you are?

- What self-identity do you wrap around yourself? How does this self-identity affect your priorities?

11

MASCULINITY VS. FEMININITY

On September 20, 1973, two tennis greats, Bobby Riggs and Billie Jean King, squared off in the Astrodome in Houston, Texas in the most-watched sporting event in history at that time. There were an estimated 90 million viewers worldwide. The event was billed as the Battle of the Sexes and was made into a feature movie in 2017. Bobby Riggs, fifty-five years old at the time, was full of bravado and was, quite frankly, the definition of a male chauvinist pig. A few months earlier he had beaten Margaret Court, a champion professional women's player, and decided there was not a woman in the world who could beat him. At the time, the twenty-nine year old Billie Jean King was the number one ranked professional women's tennis player in the world. Bobby challenged any woman in professional tennis to test their skills against his ... if they dared. Billie Jean quickly determined she had heard enough. She accepted his offer of a winner-take-all match for $100,000. Bobby needed to prove himself better than any woman and Billie Jean had to prove women could not only match men in play but deserved to match men in pay. The event was a true spectacle from the start. Billie Jean was carried on to the court in the style of Cleopatra by four bare-chested young men in the Egyptian version of a loin cloth. Bobby rode on to the court in a rickshaw pulled by several Sugar Daddy cheerleaders. After jumping out to a brief lead in the first set, Bobby fell behind and lost to Billie Jean in three straight sets. Game over.

We tend to think about masculinity vs. femininity as man vs. woman or us vs. them. Bobby Riggs attempted, unsuccessfully, to win the Battle of the Sexes to demonstrate dominance of male over female. Unfortunately, his mindset continues today and encourages society to think of women as "less than" men. This became painfully evident in the 2006 Me Too movement, protesting against sexual harassment and sexual assault committed by men against women. In 2017, #MeToo was used for the first time by Alyssa Milano to share in her personal story of being sexually assaulted. She did this in response to the headlines being made by Harvey Weinstein due to his history of sexual abuse. As a culture we've accepted this sophomoric, inappropriate, offensive, abusive, and illegal behavior and we continue to do so. This is fueled by the historical objectification of women, designed to make men feel superior and believe they're entitled to treat women with disrespect and inequality.

This is difficult for men who are more evolved to hear because it casts them in the same light with Neanderthals. In fact, many of my friends spoke to me about feeling victimized by this movement because they, of higher character, felt thrown into the same compost heap with the violators. However, from a political correctness perspective, they couldn't express this publicly for fear of their comment being misinterpreted as dismissive of women who had been violated or as a defense of the practice of harassment. Because of their gender – male – they felt guilt by association. I hope the men who are reading this are among the more evolved of our species and, if you have some Neanderthal buddies, you'll hand them a copy of this book. They need to know there is no excuse – EVER – for the types of offenses committed against women throughout history. #NeverAgain!

The perpetuated philosophy is that men are to be fully masculine and women are to be fully feminine. Men who demonstrate feminine qualities are classified as sissies, faggots, effeminate, gay, and a host of other increasingly offensive descriptors. They are excluded from the long-established Boys Club. On the other hand, women who demonstrate masculine qualities are described as butch, dikes, lesbians, bitches, and so on. Men who demonstrate feminine qualities are said to be too sensitive. Women who demonstrate masculine qualities are said to be too aggressive. The fact is, all men have masculine and feminine attributes, as do all women.

Masculinity

The word masculine is rooted in the Latin word "masculinus," which means "male-like." It's an adjective describing appearance, behavior, speech, or mannerisms. The interesting thing about this word is its prescribed expectation of normality in "being like a male." I believe there are certain innate aspects of a man's masculinity. Other aspects are developmental. Additionally, many aspects of masculinity are learned through societal and cultural norms and expectations. For example, an innate attribute of a male is the male reproductive system which develops prenatally, continues to develop in childhood, and establishes birth gender. At birth, an infant male's penis is the only thing making him appear masculine. The little boy then undergoes natural human development and achieves puberty. At puberty, testosterone levels increase and the boy undergoes physical, vocal, and behavioral change. Even if he is not taught anything of societal and cultural norms, he naturally develops human emotions and sensitivity and his hair grows long. However, there is other influence. He is taught how to be masculine. During childhood development the boy learns gender roles and what is expected of him as a male. For survival purposes he is pumped full of the modeling and teaching of appearance, behavior, speech, and mannerisms considered "normal" for a male – what is masculine. He is starved of those characteristics considered to be feminine. His acceptance and success are now based upon the strength of his masculinity and the diminishment of his femininity.

But what happened to his emotions? What happened to his sensitivity? What happened to his hair? He was taught to get rid of all of them. Successful men can't be emotional, sensitive, or have hair as long as a woman's. There you have it. Over the ages, this is what men have learned. But you cannot suppress the innate. We are created as expressive beings. Suppression of who we are at our core - our essence – leads to discontent. The little boy who cries is called a baby or a little girl. The young adult who wants to be an artist is told he needs to get a "real job" to make a living and support a family. The grown man who learned not to be vulnerable as a boy is unwilling and unable to relate to his spouse. Anything considered too feminine for male expression was purged from him.

Femininity

In my dictionary app, femininity is defined as "womanliness." Well, how are you doing with your womanliness, men?

This is exactly why men are taught to suppress emotions and sensitivity. Our society and culture have branded them as "womanly." Both men and women have both testosterone and estrogen. Does having estrogen make me womanly? No … it makes me a normal male. Does being both masculine and feminine make me womanly? No … it makes me a normal male.

Let's just put it out there that it's perfectly normal for every male to have a feminine side and take a look at it. Some typical traits of femininity include compassion, empathy, gentleness, sensitivity, healthy emotional expression, nurturing, and a focus on beauty. Let's address each of these so you can feel comfortable being both masculine and feminine:

Compassion is the regard we show and the caring we feel for another person who is in a time of struggle.

Empathy goes beyond the regard and caring we feel for another person. It includes the ability and degree to which we can relate or identify with them and their struggle.

Gentleness speaks to our ability to demonstrate patience, kindness, respect, calm, and tact in our interaction with others.

Sensitivity is recognition of the care needed in applying or releasing pressure with another person who is experiencing difficulty.

Healthy emotional expression refers to the ability to outwardly express to others what we are inwardly feeling in a healthy manner, allowing us to be functional and productive in our environment.

Nurturing is the demonstration of warmth, protection, and love toward another for the purpose of creating a bond and for teaching.

Focus on beauty refers to appreciation and attention to not only our appearance but to our surrounding environment. In terms of our physical appearance this can include hair, make-up, jewelry, dress, and physique. For environmental appearance this can include all components of design for any space within which we spend time (layout, spacing, colors, materials, lighting, and decor). This can also include a focus on the beauty of the naturally created environment.

I don't know about you, but when I look at femininity in these terms I don't feel at all like a woman. I feel like a human. I feel like a good person.

Bobby Riggs wanted to demonstrate masculine domination over femininity ... and he got his ass kicked. The truth is we need to recognize the balance of masculinity and femininity naturally existing within each of us and not allow suppression of feminine attributes. In doing so, we can be healthier versions of ourselves and better friends, partners, spouses, and fathers to those who love us exactly as we are.

Summary Points of MASCULINITY vs. FEMININITY

- All men have both masculine and feminine attributes, as do all women.

- Certain aspects of a man's masculinity are innate, some are developmental, and others are learned.

- Suppression of who you are at your core – your essence – leads to discontent.

- It is normal for every male to have a feminine side.

- Traits typically associated with femininity, also present in a healthy male, include:
  Compassion
  Empathy
  Gentleness
  Sensitivity
  Healthy emotional expression
  Nurturing
  Focus on beauty

- In order to be a better version of yourself for others, recognize the balance of masculinity and femininity naturally existing within you.

Questions for Reflection

- How have you been taught to think about masculinity vs. femininity?

- How do you view movements such as feminism or the #MeToo movement?

- Are there behaviors you've been taught to suppress to avoid a perceived threat to your masculinity? In what ways has this suppression served you well? In what ways has it been detrimental to you or those in relationship with you?

- Of the traits of femininity listed in this chapter, are there any you struggle with? If so, in what way?

12

FORGIVENESS

Ugh.

Here it is ... the chapter everyone would like to just skip. Forgiveness is hard ... really hard. It's also important. When we're unable to forgive, we carry the burden of anger, bitterness, and resentment toward somebody or some group. These negative feelings affect how we view the world, how we live our lives and, believe it or not, our mental and physical health. Forgiveness has never really been the way of the world. Even back to biblical days people were taught "an eye for an eye and a tooth for a tooth." The idea of "getting even" was considered a simple means of attaining justice. Then a radical by the name of Jesus came along and flipped that philosophy on its head. I use Jesus as my example because of where I come from spiritually, not to preach. I also believe his teachings on forgiveness and his example of granting forgiveness are unmatched. Even if you're not a Christian, see if you can agree with what Jesus, the man, taught about forgiveness and how we can weave his teachings into our own understanding.

Jesus recited what is now referred to as The Lord's Prayer, which he taught his followers to use as part of their spiritual practices. It asks God to "... forgive us our trespasses ..." In other words, he taught them to ask God to forgive their mistakes ... not just the small ones, but all of them. I guess "trespasses" could even include those things done with the knowledge they were wrong, but were done anyway. If that's the case, he was teaching them to ask for forgiveness for both mistakes and intentional wrongs. The legal term used for this today would be "torts" – " … forgive us our torts…" That plea would not likely fall well on the ears of most judges or jurors in any courtroom today. When we are wronged by others, we expect justice, not mercy. Why would Jesus tell his followers to ask for mercy instead of justice? Why would he not require them to be accountable for their wrong-doing? The answer is simple: he follows "… forgive us our trespasses" with "as we forgive those who trespass against us …"

In other words, he wanted his followers to understand they were forgiven by a gracious act. Likewise, he wanted them to show grace to others. From the Christian perspective, showing forgiveness has big implications. Holding on to anger, bitterness, or resentment creates a relational disconnect. We have a choice to either hold on to anger or to let go of it. But when we do this, we can't be selective. We have to let go of anger over all of the wrongs done to us. Holding on to any bitterness only serves to leave seeds of anger in place, allowing them to take root and grow. Jesus didn't operate from a platform of justice; he operated from a platform of mercy. This is problematic for those of us living in a world, culture, and society still demanding justice. Maybe this is because we misunderstand what forgiveness means and what it doesn't mean.

The problem with forgiveness is it's misunderstood. Some of us equate forgiveness with losing, or acceptance of a wrong. It might help if I put forgiveness into a different context so we can look at its benefits. Let's start with what forgiveness is *not* and what it does *not do*:

- *Forgiveness is not diminishing the wrong done against you* – We seem to think if we forgive a wrong, especially a big one, it minimizes what happened. It does not. The wrong done to us is by no means diminished by our decision to let go of our emotional attachment to the hurt.

- ***Forgiveness is not a denial of what happened*** – Sometimes forgiveness is equated to erasing what happened. It is not and it does not. The perpetrator of the wrong and the victim of the wrong need to acknowledge exactly what happened and not sweep it under the rug.

- ***Forgiveness does not remove consequences*** – I hear a lot of people who come to me for counseling say, "If I forgive them, they got away with it." Forgiveness is not about letting somebody off the hook. There is a cost associated with doing wrong. The cost may come in the form of a lost relationship, a loss in quality of life, repayment, serving time in jail, or many other forms. There is a cost to doing wrong.

- ***Forgiveness is not a weakness*** – "If I forgive, they win" is a common misconception. Forgiveness is not about winning and losing. Forgiveness is about moving forward and not allowing negatives to occupy a place in our own souls. Forgiveness is about pulling anger up by the root, throwing it away and allowing your life to move on, rooted in peace and love. When we look at forgiveness as exercising our own choice and making a commitment to enhance our physical, mental, emotional, and spiritual health, it is anything but weakness. It is completely empowering. On the other hand, if we make the decision not to forgive, we allow whatever hurt us in the past to continue to hurt us. The better path is to use your power of choice and commit to your self-care by letting go of anger and granting forgiveness.

- ***Forgiveness does not mean forgetting*** – "Forgive and forget." Would you do yourself a favor and *forget* this phrase? Forgive – yes. Forget – no. To forget would be opening the door to repeat offenses. It makes us vulnerable to being repeatedly mistreated, abused, or wronged. Establishing healthy boundaries is important. Failing to do so exposes us to continued wrongdoing, pain, and suffering. In essence, if we don't choose to set boundaries, we've chosen to become someone's doormat and can expect to do a lot of forgiving. This statement is not to be insensitive to anyone who was not, or is not, in control of their own environment. Children, the elderly, and those with disabilities do not choose to become someone's doormat. The need to protect and advocate for those without a voice will be discussed in Chapter 13, BOUNDARIES. We don't want to forget or deny the wrongs done to us. Healthy healing comes through the processing of these wrongs and actually *requires* they be remembered. By remembering, we're enabled to establish boundaries to prevent further injury and let go of the pain. We don't forget wrongdoing, but we choose not to allow it to have power over us or define us. By taking power away from others and what they did to us, we empower ourselves to move forward into a better quality of life.

- *Forgiveness does not wait for the offender to apologize* – Why would we want to forgive someone who hasn't apologized? There are actually a couple of very good reasons. The foremost reason is this: forgiveness is not about them - it's about us. We don't offer forgiveness for someone else to feel better about themselves. We choose to forgive so we can be healthier. If we're waiting for someone to feel bad enough about what they've done to apologize, we may carry the burden of bitterness and resentment for a long, long time. We don't need to allow someone else's pride to stand in our way of moving forward with a healthy mindset. The other reason to consider choosing forgiveness is the possibility the offender is completely unaware you were offended. This might seem unlikely to you if you've already painted the offender as a villain, but some people are truly unaware when they hurt another person's feelings. If this is the case, you're carrying anger toward a person who doesn't even know you're angry. Who does this hurt? The same question can actually be asked when you're carrying anger toward a person who does know you're angry. Who are you hurting? Your choice to forgive needs to be your choice. It is made independently of someone else's decision or their knowledge or lack of knowledge of wrongdoing. The decision to forgive – to let go - is made *by* you and *for* you. It is not earned and it may not seem fair or just, but it is merciful - not only to others but to yourself.

I think it would be inauthentic for me to argue the benefits of forgiveness without confessing a personal story of feeling wronged. It was an instance in which I felt betrayed and felt entitled to an apology. I believed forgiving would be the equivalent of sweeping the offense under the rug and excusing my offender. Because of my stance, I carried the burden of resentment and a sense of disconnectedness, preventing me from letting go and moving forward in a healthy mindset.

Many years ago I was working on a project under a contract which was being managed by a client who was also a friend. The project was challenging and several unforeseen conditions arose. They created delays and additional cost to the project which I was led to believe would be paid. At the end of the project, my friend asked me to meet him to work through all items of additional cost. When I arrived at the meeting, my friend had several people with him, including his attorney. I felt ambushed and expressed my understanding that we would be meeting alone. Needless to say the meeting did not go as smoothly as I had hoped. We were not paid for most of the costs and my company took a loss on the project. I was bitter and resentful. He moved on to another organization and I had no further communication with him for a couple of years. My resentment toward him haunted me. My anger grew heavier and heavier. Eventually, I knew I had to let it go for my own sake. I contacted my friend for a meeting and we met a couple of weeks later. I told him I carried resentment and anger toward him for the last couple of years. He was caught off guard by this. He was completely unaware I had taken things so personally and so hard. He assumed, since he hadn't heard from me, the result was satisfactory. It never entered his mind that I was too angry to speak to him. I carried bitterness and resentment for a long time toward someone who didn't even realize I was angry. Regardless of whether he felt the need for forgiveness, I told him I needed to grant it to him. In doing so, it was clear he was appreciative and gracious. What followed was a wonderful discussion and an opportunity for closure and healing. I felt I was wronged. Forgiveness required swallowing my pride, and I'm glad I did. It brought me peace and allowed me to continue in growth. I became healthier both spiritually and emotionally. Being unforgiving had me stuck and it felt good to start moving again.

As you can see, by re-examining our understanding of forgiveness we empower ourselves in many ways. We allow forgiveness to work for us rather than allowing resentment to work against us. Let's focus on what forgiveness is and what it *does* do:

- **Forgiveness is giving up your right to hurt the one who hurt you** – This may not be a very satisfying thought because of our sense of fairness. After all, we should be allowed to even the ledger, shouldn't we? What's wrong with "an eye for an eye and a tooth for a tooth"? Well … there are a couple of issues with "getting even."

  First, there's the idea of taking the high road. I'm guessing there isn't a reader of this book who hasn't heard "two wrongs don't make a right." If we're honest about it, two wrongs result in escalation of conflict. I've never heard of a situation where an offender is retaliated against and feels the retaliation was justified and appropriate in magnitude. This is not our nature. We consider the wrongs committed by us to be mistakes and the wrongs committed by others to be a result of their carelessness, thoughtlessness or, even worse, intentionality. Retaliation is not the way to resolution. Revenge does not end conflict, it extends it.

  Next, there is the mistaken idea that retaliation provides the offended with satisfaction. It doesn't. Retaliation does nothing to generate or restore relationship. The decision to retaliate instead of forgive is a decision to minimize any possibility of reconciliation. It's a decision to hold on to the sense of righteousness in hurting the one who hurt us as a means of healing. Healing and hurting are diametrically opposed. The process of healing is the discovery of a means of relief from pain. Once we experience healing we're able to move forward with experiencing the fullness of life in our present circumstances. We can experience joy and contentment despite having been hurt in the past if we are willing to let go of the pain and give up the thought that getting even will somehow be beneficial.

- *Forgiveness is an act* - I don't mean forgiveness is not real. What I mean is forgiveness is an action we take at a specific point in time. An action taken upon the decision and choice to let go. Once you've given deep thought to the wrong, the person who committed it and the benefit of giving up your resentment, you perform the act of forgiveness. It's a one-time occurrence. Once you've committed the act of forgiveness your choice should stand forever without being revisited.

- *Forgiveness is a process* – Depending upon the magnitude of the wrong and the depth of the wound, healing can take a long time. It isn't like a light switch, automatically turning off the pain and suffering associated with being wronged. The healing process of forgiveness is more like a journey. Sometimes the journey is brief. Sometimes it takes a lifetime. The point is to trust the process of healing once you've performed an act of forgiveness. In some ways, the process of forgiveness and healing can be similar to the process of grieving and healing. The road will, most likely, not be straight. The journey should not be taken alone. Talk to someone if you find yourself unable to let go. We can all use a travel companion.

There is another story – a more painful one – demonstrating what forgiveness does for us and the potential it offers for healing. The story involves an act of forgiveness, removal of my desire to "get even," and an ongoing process of healing. In 2016, my daughter Alyssa married the man she had loved for five years - a good man and a part of our family. At the beginning of 2019, he walked out on her without warning and with little explanation. Although in hindsight there may have been indicators of personal struggle, at the time there was no recognition of problems in the marriage by any of us, including Alyssa. He simply said he didn't want to be married anymore.

Devastation does not begin to describe her emotional state for the next several months. For her own emotional health she came to live with Denise and me for a while as she tried to reconcile their marriage through discussions with him and attempts at counseling. She would return home from many of these discussions and sessions and crumble … sobbing. She would talk for hours about her confusion, pain, and hope for reconciliation. Denise and I would listen, yet we were equally confused and hurt by his actions. My honest thoughts about him vacillated between praying for him and wanting to go kick his ass. I knew speaking to him about his actions and struggles was not an option. Had I attempted to do so it would have been harmful to any efforts of reconciliation between him and Alyssa. I could only sit, wait, and hope for reconciliation. Sadly, it never happened and he filed for divorce, which was finalized late in 2019. During that year I had no thoughts of forgiveness. He had hurt someone who I loved more than life itself. What helped me was knowing Alyssa is strong. As time went by, I saw her resilience, strength and resolve in moving forward. Her example of strength during her own time of healing and recovery was an example to me. I saw her working on forgiveness and realized I have no right to carry bitterness and anger if she was committed not to do so.

Once again, the teacher became the student. Alyssa caused me to think about spirituality, my faith, and what I've learned about the negative effects of unforgiveness. I thought about the struggle my former son-in-law must have been going through and the deep regret he must feel over ending the marriage in this way. He didn't mean to cause harm. He just didn't know how to seek help when he needed it. He didn't have the capacity to communicate effectively with Alyssa about what was troubling him. He is not a bad person. He is a good man who handled things very badly. I determined I needed to forgive him and I needed to let him know. I knew if I invited him to meet he would decline. I knew if I just showed up at his house he would feel trapped. I also knew my words needed to be measured carefully. I decided my best option was to write him a brief letter to let him know I forgive him, I love him and, although we no longer walk the same path, I wish him well.

It wasn't written without a lot of self-examination. I had to process a lot of pain, but it was written and it was sincere. I asked Alyssa to read the letter and asked her if it was okay for me to send it. After reading it she sat silently for a few minutes. Then she looked at me and asked, "Do you mean it?" I told her I did. She gave me permission to send it with one caveat. She asked me to wait until she met with him; she explained that she had forgiven him but had not yet told him personally. Once she had done this, the letter was sent. We both continue to go through a healing process undergirded by the undeniable power of love and forgiveness. I don't know if I will ever see or speak to him again. Despite what happened, I know, at his core, my former son-in-law is a good man and I wish him the best in life. I hope receiving forgiveness has also helped him in his healing process.

If you're stuck in unforgiveness in either a current or past relationship, consider redefining forgiveness as a means of achieving your own healing and your own joy. If you're not sure how to begin, here are a few steps to help you on the journey:

- *Acknowledge the hurt* – Don't minimize what you've experienced and don't make excuses for the offender. If it helps you to process, write your thoughts and feelings about the offense in a journal. Don't worry about spelling, grammar, punctuation, or anything you may have learned in school. Just write. It doesn't matter if you write words, phrases, sentences, or paragraphs. Be simple or be artistic. It doesn't matter how you do it – just write. Later you can reflect on the words or phrases written and go deeper into their meaning and deeper into your feelings. Journaling can be very effective in working through anger and pain. If you don't like to write, talk. Find a friend. Find a professional. Whatever you do, acknowledge the hurt.

- *Identify your emotions* – Emotional response to being hurt is normal. It's okay and necessary to claim and express your emotions. Again, journaling can be an effective tool but discussing emotions with a trusted friend who is willing to simply listen and affirm can also be helpful. I like to affirm clients by letting them know the way they feel is the way they feel – brilliant, right? This means no one has a right to say, "You shouldn't feel that way." Your feelings are your own. Let them out. Express them. Your feelings need to be acknowledged and worked through. Being emotional is okay and healthy. You'll discover by working through and examining your feelings and emotions how they protect you and are appropriate or how they are unhealthy and unhelpful. This is for you to determine and not for another person to determine for you. Your feelings and emotions are your own and you should be honest with yourself about them. Also consider being honest with others who need to hear it or can help you work through it.

- *Cancel the debt* – Write a "blank check" of forgiveness. Partially letting go is not letting go. If you're going to hang on to part of the resentment - forgiving them for "this" but not for "that" - you are not fully forgiving. This may sound harsh or critical but it's not intended to be. Writing a blank check of forgiveness is very difficult and can take a long time. If in the process of healing you've only been able to partially forgive, that's okay. But it means you're still processing the pain and there is more work to be done to reach a point of full forgiveness. You'll know when full forgiveness has occurred from the sense of inner peace you experience and the comfort you take in moving forward.

- *Set boundaries* – Decide what you need in order to protect yourself from being hurt again or from allowing an old hurt to continue impacting your ability to live life fully. Remember forgiveness does not remove consequences and it does not mean forgetting. One of the consequences for someone who inflicts pain on you is they either partially or fully lose access to you. They are not allowed to continue hurting you. The access they lose may be physical, mental, emotional, spiritual, or all of these together. It's up to you to set the boundaries in situations over which you have control.

- *Make a commitment to forgive* – Make it to yourself. Write it down. Tell yourself how you'll go about it and why you will do it. Tell yourself what unforgiveness is preventing you from doing and what forgiveness will allow you to do. The commitment is for your benefit alone and no one else's. Do this for yourself. When the time is right, let your offender know you are forgiving them even if they aren't asking for it and even if they aren't acknowledging the offense. Let them know your forgiveness comes unconditionally and you will not use your hurt as a weapon against them or try to retaliate. Let them also know it comes with protective boundaries, either limiting or cutting off their access to you. Maybe this is done face to face, over the phone, or in writing. How and when you commit to forgive is your choice.

Friends, I cannot begin to tell you how powerful and how freeing forgiveness is. I hope you will examine whatever anger, bitterness, resentment or regret you may hold toward yourself or others, consider what has been presented in this chapter, and make the choice and commitment to let it go. It will free and strengthen you more than you can possibly know.

Summary Points of FORGIVENESS

- When you are unable to forgive, you carry the burden of anger, bitterness, and resentment.

- Negative feelings affect your worldview, how you live, and your health.

- Forgiveness is a gracious act – it is about mercy, not justice.

- Forgiveness does **not** mean:
    Diminishing the wrong done to you.
    Denying what happened.
    Removal of consequences.
    Demonstration of weakness.
    Forgetting.
    Waiting for an apology.

- Forgiveness **does** mean:
    Giving up your right to hurt the one who hurt you.
    You make an intentional act of forgiveness.
    You undergo a process of healing.

- Steps to help you in the healing process of forgiveness:
    Acknowledge the hurt.
    Identify your emotions.
    Cancel the debt.
    Set boundaries.
    Commit to forgive.

Questions for Reflection

- What, in your mind, is the purpose of forgiveness?

- Who in your life have you not forgiven? What has prevented you from doing so?

- What relational disconnect do you experience due to unforgiveness?

- What might heal within you by granting forgiveness?

- What conditions have you placed on forgiveness in the past?

- How might it affect you to know you have been forgiven by someone whom you offended?

13

BOUNDARIES

In the nineties, the hit show *Seinfeld* included an episode about "close-talkers." It was a humorous depiction of a man who would violate the personal "bubble" of those he spoke with, creating a very uncomfortable situation for his bubble victims. The funny thing was, as I watched, the faces of all the close-talkers in my own life came to mind. As you read this, my guess is images of certain people come to you as well, and you recognize the reality of what Jerry Seinfeld was poking fun at. Reality makes good comedy ... and the reality is, in some way, we all have boundary issues.

Boundaries are a part of the natural order. Natural boundaries are created by the atmosphere, oceans, land, mountains, and rivers. Our ecosystem consists of boundaries affecting weather, vegetation, and every form of wildlife. All wildlife marks its territory and fiercely protects it. Boundaries are necessary for order. Boundaries are necessary for survival.

Because they are part of our natural order, boundaries have been around forever and we have learned to use them effectively. Physical boundaries are established by landmarks, placement of stones, building of fences, and construction of walls. Within peaceful settings, boundaries are established with flexibility, meaning they can be easily adjusted or crossed, within reason, without threat. In settings where a threat is perceived to exist, rigid boundaries are more likely. A good example of this is the Great Wall of China, designed and built to protect against invaders. However, an interesting thing about boundaries constructed by humans is they can act as double-edged swords. The symbolism of the Great Wall of China attests to this. It was a highly effective structure in protecting against invaders. Today it also stands as a symbol of the oppression of freedom and human rights in a country walling itself off from the outside world. The Berlin Wall, built in 1961 by the Communist government of East Germany, was a physical barrier erected to keep Western "fascists" from entering East Germany and undermining the socialist state. However, it also served to discourage mass defections from the east to the west. Overnight, this boundary separated families and loved ones from each other for decades to follow. What we desire in setting boundaries for our own lives is to create a sense of wholeness, not divisiveness. We want an improved sense of self and healthy relationships with family, friends, and co-workers. We seek freedom from having our personal bubble infringed upon either physically, verbally, or emotionally.

Good boundaries are definable, help us feel secure and worthwhile, and allow us to be aware of when they have been violated. They protect our body, property, thoughts, and emotions. However, good boundaries are not necessarily a "one size fits all" proposition. By this, I mean the boundaries we set usually depend upon how long we've known someone, how much we like them, and how much we trust them. Here are some of the good things healthy boundaries help us to do:

- Develop healthy relationships and friendships

- Enjoy true friends and family

- Respect others and avoid arguing when they say "no" to us

- Make saying "no" to others easier

- Have a strong sense of self-respect
- Share appropriate information with others
- Expect shared responsibility in relationships
- Recognize when a problem is ours and when it is someone else's
- Not tolerate disrespect or abuse

Here are some descriptors of people with healthy boundaries:

- They are secure with themselves.
- They don't let others intrude on them.
- They have a clear sense of their own views, values, and priorities.
- They're able to identify appropriate people and engage with them.
- They are confident.
- They can protect themselves without shutting themselves off.
- They know how to stand up for themselves.
- They can enter relationships without losing their own identity.
- They are able to reveal appropriate levels of information.

Seeing these attributes of people with good boundaries makes it apparent they will more likely experience the freedom to pursue a life of joy and contentment. Part of achieving this joy and contentment is knowing how to apportion the access we give to others. Obviously, there are those who we will allow to be close to us, such as our family, friends, or partners. However, even those we allow closest to us may not have the same level of access. For example, the physical or emotional intimacy toward a friend may not be the same shown toward a spouse or partner. For friends and family we may allow more flexibility with our boundaries. On the other hand, we may need our boundaries to be much more secure and rigid with others. Those who have been abusive or threatening toward us in any way should lose access to us, partially or completely, and only have it restored if and when they can be trusted. There are obviously many levels of access we can allow others to have to us physically. These range on a scale of no access at all to complete access. You are the decision-maker regarding who is allowed access and how much they are allowed.

Discussion of boundaries can really be tough because they can also carry a lot of emotion. For the parent whose adolescent child or adult child is struggling with addiction or alcohol abuse and is unable to function in relationships, school, or at work, decisions are difficult. Having no boundaries or loose boundaries (not properly protecting us or those in our care) can enable whatever problem exists to either remain or worsen. This can be financially, emotionally, and physically draining to those who cannot set healthy boundaries. On the other hand, rigid boundaries – in this case, tough love – might involve re-moving every form of financial or material support from the adoles-cent or adult child until they make their own decision to seek help and get sober.

This could even include removing them from your home. I spoke with a mother who described this as the most gut-wrenching deci-sion she and her husband ever had to make. They knew setting a rigid boundary with their struggling son was the only way for them and their other children to live a healthy life. They also knew this could, potentially, result in his death. Their love for their son never wavered. Nor did their desire for his well-being. Nevertheless, after repeated attempts to help him through recovery, they made the most difficult decision imaginable to a parent and put him out of the house. As a parent I cannot imagine how emotionally devastating this decision, the last chance for his survival, must have been for them. I am thank-ful to say, because of their love for him and the boundary they were willing to establish, he has survived and thrived. Sadly, this is not al-ways the case. Had they enabled him to continue down the path he was on or had he made the decision to stay on the streets, his story may have ended differently. I encourage parents of children who abuse drugs to seek out professional counselors for guidance in treatment. Boundaries can be tough, but they're necessary for order and survival.

Establishing effective boundaries depends a lot on how much we depend upon the approval of others. The greater the need for approval and acceptance, the more difficult it is to set healthy boundaries for ourselves. I've already spoken of the need to evaluate the influence those around you have on your life. This evaluation, in and of itself, is not helpful without self-actualization. This means you need to have self-esteem, self-confidence, self-determination, and the commitment to self-care. You don't need to continue to seek the approval of people who harm you mentally, physically, or emotionally. In setting your boundaries, surround yourself with those who build you up and affirm your value. Distance yourself from those who don't.

I see those with the need for acceptance and approval struggle with the internal emotions of distancing themselves from the unhealthy people in their lives. They can't place a boundary between themselves and those who hurt them because they might lose the acceptance they so desperately desire. There is usually a deeply rooted motivation for approval and acceptance. This motivation will vary from person to person, but it will result in a people-pleasing tendency which disregards their own needs. If you have been pursuing the approval of those who create toxicity in your life, I urge you to start acting on your own behalf. If you consider this selfish, think of how allowing others to take advantage of you is enabling them to be self-absorbed at your expense. Self-care is not selfish. Self-care is healthy for you and demonstrates the respect you have for yourself. It also establishes the standard of respect you expect from others. The reverse is also true – if you disrespect yourself, you can expect others to show you disrespect. Act on your own behalf. Take care of your own physical, mental, and emotional needs. In setting boundaries, respect yourself. In doing so, you will be teaching others about respecting you as well. Stand up for yourself. You can start with your electronic devices. Block calls and texts from those who are caustic. Unfriend or unfollow those who create resentment. You can also consider protecting your time. Dedicate your time to those you love and respect and to those who demonstrate love and respect for you. Don't give your time away to those who only want to argue, accuse, diminish, manipulate, and take advantage of you. You don't have to be a martyr.

Let's also consider the boundaries we establish in how we treat our own bodies. We can treat our bodies in healthy or unhealthy ways and it's for us to determine what we will allow. We need to make decisions regarding what we put into our bodies - what we eat, what we drink, and the chemicals or medications we use. We need to make decisions regarding exercise – our capacity, how much is desired, and what is beneficial. We need to make decisions related to recreational activity – consider physical and medical risks or rewards and whether or not protection is warranted. We need to decide how much sleep we intend to get each night. All of these personal decisions are for the purpose of establishing healthy limits or boundaries. Take a look at how you treat yourself. Take a look at how others treat you. Decide whether your current boundaries are helping you or harming you and make the necessary changes.

For those of you who are caregivers to the defenseless, setting and guarding their boundaries is especially important. In Chapter 12, FORGIVENESS, I said you can become a doormat if you lack healthy boundaries. I also said those who are not in control of their own situations and who are in the care of others (children, those with disabilities, and the elderly) don't have the ability to set their own boundaries. If you are a parent or a caregiver caring for someone who is defenseless against abuse, use all due diligence to minimize the possibility of their victimization. Set the boundaries on their behalf and set them firmly. This means background checks and personal interviews for any who will be providing any level of care in your absence. This means empowering those in your care to say whether or not they want to be touched. This includes whether or not they want to give a hug goodbye or a hug goodnight to a relative. If they don't want to, they don't have to. It is important for them to have a voice regarding their own body. If this is embarrassing to you, make whatever excuse you need to make - but give honor and respect to their choice. You have to get over your own embarrassment, assuring those in your care remain safe. Also…*believe those in your care if they say they have been violated or harmed in any way* – verbally, physically, or emotionally. Even if you can't imagine they are telling the truth, give them the benefit of the doubt for their own protection. Remove them from the potentially harmful environment and file a report to appropriate authorities – no matter if the possible perpetrator is a relative or a friend. The bottom line is this – those who do not have the capacity to set their own boundaries must be protected to the greatest degree possible by the boundaries put in place for them by their caregivers. Even if an investigation discloses no wrongdoing, it is better to err on the side of caution when it comes to those who cannot care for themselves. It's unfortunate I should even have to include this paragraph, but my previous experience as a counselor of children and adolescents who have suffered sexual abuse has taught me the stark reality of our need to protect those who cannot protect themselves.

A lack of boundaries can lead to repeated victimization. If you're being victimized by your own unhealthy boundaries and you have the ability to get this under control, you and you alone are responsible for doing so. If someone in your care has the potential to be victimized due to poor boundaries, you and you alone are responsible for creating healthy boundaries for them. Whether setting boundaries for yourself or as a caregiver to someone else, please evaluate and act on establishing healthy boundaries today. Unhealthy boundaries can lead to serious issues in our lives and the lives of others. While we might be able to laugh at Seinfeld's close-talker, in truth, there is nothing funny about poor boundaries or boundaries that are violated.

Summary Points of BOUNDARIES

- Boundaries are necessary for order and survival.

- Boundaries can be flexible or rigid, according to your needs.

- Boundaries can protect us, but they can also isolate us.

- Boundaries should create a sense of personal wholeness.

- Boundaries are definable.

- Boundaries are not a "one size fits all" proposition.

- Boundaries enhance your freedom to experience a life of joy and contentment.

- You are the decision-maker regarding who has access to you and how much access you provide.

- Healthy boundary setting requires self-esteem, self-confidence, self-determination, self-care, self-respect and self-actualization.

- Establish boundaries for yourself regarding nutrition, sleep, and exercise. What priority will you give to your physical health?

- Caregivers must set firm boundaries for the protection of those in their care.

- A lack of healthy boundaries can result in personal violation and victimization.

Questions for Reflection

- Have you ever had a boundary of yours violated? How did you know it was violated? What effect did it have on you?

- How have healthy boundaries helped you?

- How have unhealthy boundaries hurt you?

- How do you set boundaries differently for different people?

- How much ease or struggle do you experience in setting appropriate boundaries? Why do you consider boundary setting easy or difficult?

- How can you begin today to set healthy boundaries for yourself or for someone in your care?

14

SPIRITUALITY

The legendary football coach of the Texas Longhorns, Darrell Royal, once said this about passing the football:

> "Three things can happen when you pass the ball, and two of them are bad. You can catch the ball, you can throw it incomplete, or have it intercepted."

Perhaps the same thing can be said of discussing spirituality. You can be in agreement, you can be in disagreement, or you can create conflict. While none of these are necessarily bad, a couple of them can be uncomfortable.

Because spirituality is such a personal matter, many people are uncomfortable discussing it at all. We don't want to offend and we don't want conflict. As a result, we avoid talking about one of the very things core to our existence. Much of the time this is because we equate spirituality with religion, yet they are distinctly different. I know some religious people who are not spiritual. They use their religion like a weapon rather than allowing it to transform their hearts of stone to hearts for love and mercy. These are the people who dissuade others from being comfortable with religion. Thankfully, I know many more who are both religious and spiritual – living into the teachings of their religion and having love and compassion for others. Then there are the spiritual people who are not religious. I've heard some religious people say spirituality without religion is a cop out. I disagree. Spirituality can be experienced outside of religion. However, any form of spirituality requires acknowledgment of a Higher Power through which we are sustained and strengthened. Your spiritual belief may be in one God, many gods, or no God at all. Your spiritual belief may be founded on nature, energy, karma, or just living right. If you're a religious person your spirituality may be based upon the teachings of Christianity, Islam, Gnosticism, Judaism, Hinduism, Buddhism, Shintoism, or any other "ism." Even skepticism. Whatever yours may be, we all have a belief related to spirituality. I have mine. You have yours. They are most likely different even if they are the same.

This chapter is important because we often go through life on auto-pilot when it comes to our own spirituality. The reason I've included it as the last chapter is this: *spirituality is the most important aspect of who we are.* It is the best subject on which to anchor everything else discussed in this book. There is also another reason. If you are a skeptic, the subject of spirituality or religion as an opener may have scared you away before you even started your journey of self-examination. I hope by now I've earned your trust in presenting this information in a manner safe to you, regardless of your current spiritual beliefs. The spiritual journey is just too important for any of us to miss. I'd like to start by telling you about my own journey and the life "markers" affecting it up to this point. As I do, I invite you to consider your own spiritual journey, the markers in your life, and where you find yourself today.

I grew up in the Catholic Church, following its traditions, its sacraments, and its rituals from the time I was born until I went off to college. I did this not because I had any particular attachment to its beliefs but because my family was Catholic … my dad's family was Catholic … my grandfather's family was Catholic. You get the picture - my family's Catholic roots go way back. I started to resist going to church when I was in high school but was still required to go - so I went, begrudgingly.

I still remember the detailed and developed argument I presented to my parents for not attending church in my adolescence: "It's stupid." They gave my argument its due consideration and provided their rebuttal: "Get in the car, we're going to church."

Faith became less stupid for me when I was invited by a good-looking girl to a youth organization called YoungLife, which was far different from any form of church I had attended in my own young life. In the YoungLife environment I was more open to what was being said, personalized more of what was being taught, and started my own spiritual journey in earnest. After high school I went to college and, like many, forgot about (or so I thought) anything YoungLife had taught and anything about a spiritual journey.

In my senior year I met my wife-to-be, Denise. She had grown up in Army chapels, primarily Protestant, and remained involved in church through high school and sporadically through college ... voluntarily! When we married, she was both vocal and intentional about her desire to resume regular church attendance. After a one-year delay on my part (due to my struggle with attending anything other than a Catholic Church), my Catholic guilt caught up with me for not attending worship with Denise. I decided to attend a Presbyterian Church with her - even though I knew God didn't live there.

Note: If you are now an offended Presbyterian, please understand I have a dry sense of humor and certainly intended no harm.

*Note: If, even after reading my first note of disclaimer, you are **still** an offended Presbyterian, take satisfaction in the thought that, just perhaps, I didn't make the predestination cut list. Once again ... dry sense of humor.*

In attending church with Denise, I learned a lot about myself and my preconceived ideas about other churches. As a result, I was able to begin an eye-opening journey regarding both religion and spirituality. Denise and I grew in faith and grew to love our church family.

As we began our own family, we committed to be in church every Sunday. Although my work required us to move several times over the years, finding a church home was always a first priority. Fellowship with others gave us and our daughters a sense of spiritual community and connection. It allowed us to learn, grow, and develop deeper understanding of our own faith and spirituality. This comes through asking questions, challenging beliefs, and being open to the reality that none of us have all the answers, even if we know what we believe. The healthy question is, "Why do I believe what I believe?"

Now let's turn to your spiritual journey. As you've read about mine, which is far from finished, what thoughts about your journey have come to mind? Maybe it all sounds to you like something for weak-minded people and you've got no interest. That's fine. However, I would ask this: If that's the case, why did you start the chapter and why are you continuing to read? I think the answer to this lies in the assumption that we are all looking for answers and we are all looking for a sense of connection to something. I hope you will continue reading (you've made it this far!) and looking for your spiritual connection. It is life changing.

Some of you might be reflecting on the possibility of a Higher Power outside of organized religion. If this is the case, good for you! Organized religion is only a by-product of specific faith beliefs created by human beings and for human beings to develop a better and deeper understanding of a Higher Power and its intersection and/or intervention in our lives. You don't have to join a church to appreciate or believe in a Higher Power. Even Jesus admonished the "church" leaders of his day for losing sight of what is Godly when they created rules and obstacles preventing the spiritual growth and connectedness of the people. Church as we know it today can be very complicated. While it has been a tremendous source of growth, learning, and understanding for me, I recognize it has been a source of pain and suffering for many. This is not because of a Higher Power. This is because of human beings acting the way human beings act ... imperfectly. Even if you reject the church, I urge you to continue exploring your spirituality and spiritual connection with others.

Some of you experience your spirituality through nature. This might include observation and/or study of trees, rivers, earth, rocks, wildlife, planets, stars, galaxies, or the universe as a whole. What a beautiful experience it is to be far from the city lights and look up to "the heavens" and experience its vastness in comparison to our limitedness. It is a humbling and spiritual experience. In that moment of wonder, contemplation of how it all came to be is proof of the limitedness of our understanding. It is fodder for further spiritual exploration. We want a sense of connection to our universe and to others. It brings peace to think about the natural order of creation. Even as I sit in this moment writing my thoughts of nature and spirituality, I sense the gaze of my black lab, Emma, and feel the connection she desires with me. Perhaps she is guiding me to a deeper understanding and experience of spirituality and connection. Could her gaze be communicating the universal connectedness desired by the Higher Power and Creator of all – the one I call God? As I consider this further, it's also possible she's just waiting to be fed.

Spiritual Practices

Exploring spirituality alone is, well – lonely – and difficult. If you don't know where to start, do some research on different forms of spiritual practices. This can include everything from attending worship to reading books and talking to others who are also on a spiritual journey - people who might be able to provide you with insight and guidance. Described below are several different spiritual practices you might find helpful:

Prayer

Prayer may seem like a waste of time to some people. And if they are praying to nothing, they would be right. Why pray to something you don't believe in or don't believe exists? In Chapter 12, FORGIVENESS, I wrote about the difficult year my daughter Alyssa had in 2019 due, in part, to the end of her marriage. But it didn't end there. She found herself angry with God because she didn't hear or feel a response to her prayers for her marriage. Toward the end of the year I asked her how she was doing spiritually. She replied, "God and I are no longer on speaking terms." While I could understand and appreciate this, these were still difficult words for me to hear. They indicated the depth of the pain of abandonment she felt … first by her husband and then by her God. But it didn't end there. At 9:00 p.m. on October 20, 2019 several tornadoes touched down, causing mass destruction in the Dallas area. Alyssa happened to be driving home from work at the time. She called us at 9:04 p.m., stunned but coherent. One of the tornadoes crossed the interstate at the exact moment she was driving on that section of the highway. The tornado hit her car as she drove, shattered all of the windows, and lifted and spun the car, severely damaging the body and blowing out all four of the tires. What she was telling us was absolutely unimaginable, almost as unimaginable as the fact that she escaped without injury … and with her sense of humor intact. First, she told us what happened and then said, "But there's good news." I asked her, other than being alive, what the good news could possibly be. She responded, "I'm talking to God again."

We all need to believe there is something greater than ourselves when we are in crisis. Sometimes we don't truly know what we believe until the crisis hits. But why wait until then? Prayer is our opportunity to talk with a Higher Power at any time. It connects us with a recharging energy source when our own battery is low and it allows us to express thanks when we feel filled. If you don't pray, I encourage you to start. Don't worry about the right way or the wrong way. Just do it how and when it feels right to you without any self-judgment or self-condemnation. This might mean once a day for some and throughout the day for others. It's okay … just connect to the Higher Power in your own meaningful way. If you're worried about getting answers …

don't be. Just talk. Because when you really think about it, prayer is not about achieving results. It's about connection and transformation. It's about connecting with a Higher Power than ourselves and being transformed by the knowledge and acceptance that we are created for love and out of love.

Meditation

Does this sound a little too "Zen" for you? If you've ever uttered the words or thought to yourself "I wish I could just get away from all of this for a little while," here is your chance. Meditation is an act of devout spiritual contemplation and introspection, allowing you to briefly retreat from the hamster wheel of life. It is the opportunity for you to empty your mind of all its daily traffic and to allow a spiritual Energy to pour over you. If prayer is about transmitting, then meditation is about receiving. As with communication in our human relationships, most of us are much better at transmitting than receiving. Prayer is an opportunity to share your heart's desires and meditation is an opportunity to quiet your minds. This is what makes meditation difficult. To demonstrate the difficulty in quieting your mind, humor me for a moment. I'd like you to sit quietly for sixty seconds and think about nothing but the air you're breathing in and out. Ready? Go.

(Pause for a sixty-second breathing meditation.)

How did it feel? Did it seem like an eternity? Did you have distracting thoughts or sounds?

We live in an environment where we're expected to be productive at home, work, and school. There's an endless "to do" list for us....well...to do. In a society and culture where being busy is thought to be better, meditation is definitely considered by many as nonproductive. In my opinion, meditation may be the most productive thing you do in a day. It helps you to clear your mind, become more focused, and be more productive in accomplishing the things that matter. When studying for my National Counseling Exam I used several resources. Every one of them mentioned the importance of taking study breaks because, at a certain point, our minds become saturated and cannot retain further information. I found this to be very true. But I still had to fight the urge to continue, cram, stay up late, and worry about what test content I hadn't studied adequately. In the same way, your brain can become "locked" without breaks. You need to take breaks at work, home, and school or you become overwhelmed … always doing but never done. Meditation is a break. It helps you to be more productive with higher quality in what you produce.

Meditation is also a spiritual practice. To sit quietly and empty our minds of everything allows us to experience an omni-present and omni-powerful energy. The longer we're able to sit in a meditative state, the more the presence of Energy can be felt and the more deeply we are able to experience it. I can say this because I have experienced it. Initially, meditation was difficult for me and filled with distractions. I started meditating for just a few minutes and, as I became more proficient at dismissing unwelcome thoughts, I would increase the time. The more time I spent in meditation, the more effective it was and the more peaceful I felt. I was clearer about what mattered and what didn't matter and became less prone to allow unimportant distractions to prevent me from what I needed to do.

I believe meditation will do the same for you. Consider starting your day with a five-minute meditation. You might do it in silence and focus on breathing. Meditative music can also be helpful in blocking out distracting thoughts or sounds. You might even use a mantra of your choosing – words for you to focus on. Just find a place where you can be alone and with as few distractions as possible and give it a try. I think it will make a big difference in your day and in your spirituality.

Scripture

Be it the Quran, the Torah, the Bible, or another form of spiritual writings, scripture can enrich our spiritual growth. The reading and study of scripture can open our minds to the thoughts and experiences of people throughout documented history and their understanding of relationship to a Higher Power. The scripture I choose to read, study, discuss, and debate is the Bible. It includes stories of creation and salvation, love, war, human interaction with God, God's interaction with humans, proverbs, poetry reflecting hope, and poetry reflecting hopelessness. In short, it reflects the human experience and the opportunity to see ourselves as reflected in the stories of others. It is spiritually inspired writing, attempting to help humans better understand and relate to God and to each other. I like to refer to these areas of understanding and relationship as vertical (with God) and horizontal (with others). Scripture helps us learn, understand, and be in relationship vertically and horizontally, creating a "plus" sign, or a positive in our lives. Without positive relationships, vertically and horizontally, we cannot experience the fullness of life.

Books on Spirituality and Faith

In addition to scripture, I find it helpful to read other books on spirituality and faith. These books can provide deeper spiritual understanding and a fresh perspective regarding our own faith and the faiths of others. I think it is important to read books challenging to our beliefs and not just those supportive of our current beliefs or understandings. There should be no fear in this. Our beliefs are formed and solidified through this process of answering challenges in an informed and thoughtful manner. We must be solidly grounded not only by what we were taught as children but based on what we have considered as adults.

I also enjoy reading on spirituality and faith from the perspective of great leaders. Some of these leaders are from the business world, such as Ken Blanchard, and some are great historical figures, such as Dietrich Bonhoeffer. Other areas for growth and understanding can come from biographies of those with great faith, such as Abraham Lincoln, Martin Luther King Jr., and William Wilberforce. These books inspire us. They cause us to question what more we can do to "Love our neighbor" or, perhaps, to evaluate the false limitations we have placed on our ability to do so.

The bottom line is this … leaders are readers. If you want to be inspired and be inspiring, read. If you want to grow in your spirituality and faith, read. If you want to set a great example for your children, nieces, nephews, or any others who look up to you, read. If you want to boost your self-confidence, read. Who knows? Reading may one day inspire you to write.

Writing

Isn't it interesting what you find people posting on social media sites? I often think after reading someone's post, "I would never post that" or "They wouldn't say that to someone's face." This supports the argument that sometimes we won't say what we're willing to write. Because we sometimes have thoughts we can't or, for some reason, shouldn't verbalize or emote, writing our thoughts through a safe outlet can be of therapeutic and spiritual benefit.

The spiritual practice of writing is a truly freeing experience. In a private journal you can choose to write whatever you want. You can write what you're thinking and what you're feeling without worrying about what is said or how it is said. You don't have to worry about spelling or grammar. You don't have to worry about sentence structure. Journaling gives you free rein and artistic license in word expression. This is important because for certain experiences there are no words … only deep-seated feelings or emotions. Journaling allows us to express, sometimes nonsensically, what we don't know how to say. I believe these written utterances are like a prayer. There are times when our feelings of joy or sorrow can only be shared with a Higher Power in which we can trust. We can write and have confidence that, regardless of the quality or sensibility of our words, we are understood. Ultimately, isn't being understood a desire everyone shares?

Likewise, we can express ourselves in writing through poetry, songs, and literature. In these forms of writing there is a message to be communicated. Our attempt is to do so in a meaningful and inspiring way. The very word "inspire" means to breathe in. The idea of spirituality being expressed through every breath we take as created beings is what moves us to be creative. This Divine inspiration, received through every breath, allows us to create meaning for ourselves and others. Spiritually inspired writing provides clarity and insight for our own lives and can help provide understanding for others. The process of creative writing seems, at first, a daunting task. Starting is the hardest part, but the journey becomes smoother as thoughts begin to flow and you find a natural and inspired order to your words. Who knows … someday the thoughts you put into words for your own benefit may be published for the benefit of others.

Art

Art is expressed in countless ways. I've been moved by writing, songs, photographs, dance, paintings, sculptures, carvings and, I'm sure, many other forms of art. I've come to believe there is no such thing as "good" or "bad" art. Instead, there are forms of art some people prefer to others.

As part of the service in the church where I worship, there is occasionally a performance of liturgical dance presented by a local dance studio. This is primarily made up of a group of middle schoolers and high schoolers. I must confess, when I first heard they would be performing as a part of worship I envisioned a bad recital being inserted into the middle of our worship service. I could not have been more wrong. From their first performance I came to appreciate the spirituality of their gift of dancing. It was evident in their eyes, expressing full adoration for their Creator. It was demonstrated in the choreography and the unity of their graceful movement. It was present in the material of their costumes, flowing as though supported by the movement of the Holy Spirit around the entire troupe. Maybe I struggled with dance as a spiritual expression because it's not my own gift. But I could see in the movement of these young people the deeply meaningful expression of their spirituality … and I have been blessed by it.

Art which is not part of a worship service can be equally spiritual to the art of dance mentioned above. The artist in my family is my sister, Jude. I'm amazed at the creativity, vision, and inspiration she has for producing something beautiful from a blank canvas. The eyes of the women she paints are soul-bearing and the colors she creates are vibrant. They reflect the spirituality, mystery, and soul of a Higher Power speaking through each of us in unique and powerful ways.

I may have been born with two left feet and I may consider stick figures to be the extent of my artistic ability, but the spirit within me is inspired by the spirituality and the giftedness of others. We all have unique gifts and talents. I encourage you to work on finding your art and using it as a means of spiritual expression for yourself and others.

Small Groups

I speak a lot about connectedness to others because it has been very meaningful to my own spiritual development. We are not created for isolation. Isolation will lead to loneliness, depression, or stagnation. Even the deepest introvert occasionally needs to have human contact – trust me on this!

As I write, the Coronavirus Pandemic of 2020 is being felt globally. Many counties, states, and countries have issued a "Shelter in Place" order or, at minimum, are recommending social distancing. "Social distancing" - the virus is so powerful it created new terminology. We can remain connected via social media, but it's just not the same as being with a real flesh-and-blood person. We're not comforted because we aren't meant to live this way. We aren't meant to stand six feet away from each other as part of being in community. Community is important and groups within community are important. Don't misunderstand me - the social distancing required during the pandemic was necessary and appropriate for the protection of the individuals within our communities whose systems are immunocompromised. Although it was necessary, social distancing also caused me to be increasingly aware of how much I missed and needed personal connection. Social distancing allowed me to understand how loving and caring for my community can sometimes involves personal sacrifice.

I've mentioned several times the importance of having an accountability group. This is a group of trusted individuals with whom you are safe being vulnerable with your innermost struggles, thoughts, joys, or fears. They should be like mentors who will hold you accountable and call you on your B.S. – and you're not offended when they do!

For me, Sunday School and Bible Study classes are central to my spiritual growth and fellowship. Both my Sunday School and Bible Study are "all male" classes. I have nothing at all against co-ed classes, and have been a member of many, but men express themselves differently and more freely when they are with other men. In other words, we don't burn as many brain cells searching for politically correct language. We do, however, try to provide wise counsel to each other in using political correctness outside of the classroom! Whether you are with other men or with men and women, don't miss the opportunity to participate in a small group. The relationships you build and the growth you will experience will last you a lifetime and make you a better friend, partner, husband, or father.

By the way ... due to the coronavirus, my small groups are all meeting online at this point. Online groups may have been forced upon us by the virus, but I believe they will actually be beneficial for many individuals as we move forward. If you can't have a person-to-person group, consider forming your own online group. Just stay connected – it's important.

Worship

Worship brings us together and gives us an opportunity to be inspired. It's a time set apart for us to connect with both God and people, the vertical and horizontal connections critical to our spiritual health.

I think along these lines – if we don't have a strong and authentic connection to our Higher Power, we can't have a strong and authentic connection with others. I believe we need both to live a fulfilled life. To offer our hearts collectively to our Higher Power through words, song, and prayer is a spiritual practice which strengthens community. Through worship, life becomes about what we have in common as opposed to what divides us.

In the traditional liturgical form of worship, we're given a message from a leader of the people. Different religions have varying titles for them, but what these leaders generally have in common is dedication to the study, principles, and beliefs of the faith they represent. These men and women devote themselves to our collective Higher Power. They live out their faith, understanding what it means to live in community and harmony in this delicately balanced yet widely expansive creation. Their messages are inspired through their own spiritual practices. They pray, write, read, study, meditate, worship, and commune with others. They are inspired by all of these practices, as well as their own experiences. Through these practices and their experienced life as created beings, they speak to us through God-breathed words – inspired by both creation and the Creator. Their words are designed to move us. They motivate us to live in a way which honors both humanity and the Higher Power. Their messages provide wisdom in helping us do so.

When we hear the word worship, many of us think about a certain day, time, and place where we go each week for the purpose of a liturgical experience. While there is value in this practice for establishing consistency and community, it is not the only form of worship. Worship can be done and experienced anywhere and anytime. While the words and messages from our faith leaders are inspiring and provide guidance for living, I believe nature allows us to hear unspoken messages. In natural settings we can also hear and experience the message of the Creator. Think of a time when you were alone with nature. Close your eyes and recall the sounds of water, birds, wind, rustling leaves, the call of an animal ... or complete silence. Feel the warmth or the chill of the air. Feel the wind or notice the stillness. Feel the grass, the sand, or the rock on which you stood. See the valley, the mountain, or the ocean in front of you. Think of your part in the delicate balance of it all. There is an unspoken message and wisdom we can receive from the Higher Power if we allow our senses to experience worship anywhere we go.

Communion

Communion is a spiritual practice unique to the Christian faith. While some denominations limit this spiritual practice to their own church members, the communion table in my denominational tradition is open to all who wish to partake in this sacrament. Because this is my belief, I include this spiritual practice for all to consider. This practice is based on the Biblical scripture found in the book of Luke, chapter 22, verse 19, where Jesus shared the Passover meal with his apostles for the last time and instructed them to continue in this tradition of breaking bread together. Today, communion serves as a reminder of Jesus' ministry and the sacrifice he made for all of humanity. For those of us who follow the teaching and instruction of Jesus, we believe he was God represented to humanity and one who lives on in Spirit. Communion is remembrance of the connection we have today and eternally with Jesus, with God, and with the Spirit dwelling within each of us. It should motivate us to live in community and in harmony with each other and to love God, love our neighbor, and love ourselves. In doing these things we give honor to Jesus and remember the price he paid – death on a cross – for us to experience the eternal peace and joy (on earth and forever after) which he referred to as the Kingdom of Heaven. It is very meaningful not only to take communion but to observe others doing the same. To take communion and observe others doing so is, for me, a sacred moment. It's a time of unity and a time to consider what we have in common – the love of Jesus. Communion can be received as a part of a worship service or outside of a worship service. Either way, depending upon your faith tradition, there may be specific procedures to observe in the blessing of the elements (bread and wine/grape juice) and the receiving of communion. Wherever it is done and however it is done it is, in itself, an act of worship and a meaningful spiritual practice.

Confession

Because I grew up Catholic, the word "confession" evokes a very specific memory of going into a little cubbyhole at the church to tell a priest on the other side of the screen everything I'd done wrong since I had last visited the cubbyhole. There was almost always something to confess. If there wasn't, I'd make something up for the appearance of needing penance. If nothing else, it gave the priest something to do.

I obviously didn't take confession too seriously when I was younger, but as I grew older and recognized the weight of the conflict and struggle I carried with me, I came to understand its value. If your tradition is making confession to a priest and you're comforted and unburdened by this practice, it's certainly what I'd recommend for you. However, I want to address confession on a broader scale and take the sting out of the "churchy" terminology. How about if, instead of "confession," I just refer to it as the need to get something off your chest. You may find it to be more of a private matter and make it a part of your own talks with God. On the other hand, you may find no comfort at all in the idea of sharing struggles with a Higher Power. In either case, it's fair to say that we've all done things we're not proud of. We all have things we struggle with. Use whatever terminology you want to for what you've done or what you're dealing with. The bottom line is this - if it's bothering you, it's probably worth talking about with someone you trust. Getting things off your chest can be spiritually freeing and eliminate the isolation felt over the "dirty secrets" you feel the need to protect.

Reiki Therapy

We tend to think of the human body in terms of flesh and bone. But we're much more. Our central nervous system, which controls every bodily function, is a series of millions of electrical circuits. It's made up of nerve fibers consisting of neurons, each of which has axons and dendrites. Nerve fibers function by picking up signals from the environment through sight, sound, smell, and touch. They electronically transmit and receive these signals between neurons through the "firing" of axons and dendrites. All of this is done in milliseconds. This process is what causes your foot to immediately step on the brake when your eyes suddenly see an object appear in front of you. The science of human development reveals that we are literally a bundle of nerves! But what does any of this have to do with spiritual practices?

Reiki therapy is a Japanese technique of healing based upon the knowledge that our bodies are, in essence, energy. In fact, the word Reiki is derived from the two Japanese words "Rei", which means "God's wisdom/Higher Power" and "Ki", which means "life force energy." In Reiki therapy, the therapist lays hands on or above the body at various known energy centers, called Chakras. Through this process, healthy and unhealthy areas of the body can be identified. Therapists can then speak to possible causes of low energy, suggest practices for improvement (such as nutritional or physical changes), and help us to heal. I can attest to the effectiveness of Reiki therapy as a spiritual practice because I have experienced its effect.

There may be a few of my Christian friends who are rolling their eyes at this. If so, consider the Christian belief that we are made in God's image. If God is the energy behind all creation and we are made in God's image, then we ourselves are energy. In this sense, scripture reveals the same human development as science. We are created as a result of energy and, through energy, our central nervous system develops and functions. Without energy we cease to exist. I offer this to you as a spiritual practice if you are able to wrap your head around the concept of God as energy, as the word "Reiki" denotes, and yourself as created in the image of God.

Gratefulness

It's very difficult to have an attitude of gratefulness and resentment at the same time. What you choose to focus on determines your thoughts, actions, and attitude. Which attitude would you prefer to focus on? Which attitude would you prefer to be around?

Gratefulness requires our intentional focus on the blessings of life. We have so much provision to be thankful for. We are provided strength to overcome obstacles. We are provided relationships through which we are encouraged and loved. We are provided resources for survival. We are provided skill sets enabling us to work. We are provided beauty for comfort. We are provided community for support. We are provided nature for inspiration. When we consider the Divine interaction in all creation, "awe" is the only word brought to mind. When we consider the intricate and delicate balance of nature, we can only have awe and gratitude for the Higher Power bringing it all into being. Our gratitude should cause us to be good stewards of the gift of creation we are given. As I ponder such a generous Creator, I can only be grateful.

We too often neglect the spiritual practice of gratefulness. This is generally true in our relationship with others as well as in our relationship with the Creator. Our human tendency is to focus on what we don't have, what we want, or getting "more." Focusing on what we don't have causes us to miss what we do have. Focusing on gratefulness means we both recognize blessings received and acknowledge them with thankfulness. In America, we've set aside one day of the year to do this. Wouldn't it be nice if every day was Thanksgiving Day? If we could dedicate ourselves to being grateful every day, imagine our change in attitude. Imagine how this would enable us to focus on what unites us instead of what divides us. Imagine how our eyes would be opened to all of the good around us. Imagine how our attitudes toward others who don't look, think, or act like us might change. Imagine replacing inner turmoil with inner peace. Perhaps the best thing of all is this – when we focus on gratefulness we are also more likely to adopt an attitude of generosity.

Generosity

As I write, the world enters into Holy Week, the week on the Christian calendar representing Jesus' entry into Jerusalem, his capture, his death on the cross and, ultimately, his resurrection. In the pastor's Palm Sunday message, he focused on Jesus and the generosity represented by his life and in his death. The pastor referred to Jesus' generosity as an example of a spiritual practice for us. I recognized the truth in this and was inspired to add this section. All we have to do is look around to recognize what we've been given. The gift of connection, the gift of creation, and the gift of simply "being" are all examples of experienced generosity from the Creator. Our likeness to this Creator would suggest we are created for generosity toward each other – a spiritual practice. Generosity comes in many forms – sharing of time, finances, talents and gifts, to name a few. I would encourage you to examine where, when, and to whom generosity is displayed in your life. It may be volunteering at a soup kitchen, a thrift store, or any non-profit organization. It may be reading to school children, visiting nursing homes or with those who are unable to leave their homes. It may be helping a neighbor with yard work or home maintenance. What about generosity in your own home and in your own relationships? How are you being generous with your spouse, partner, children, parents, or siblings? We tend to think of generosity in terms of what we do in the community, which is very important. However, the generosity shown at home is critical to relationship. One example of generosity is to teach generosity. If you have children or nieces and nephews, teach them generosity in every possible area of their lives. If you volunteer, take them with you. If you donate money or articles, tell them why this is important. Generosity may be one of the most significant and impactful of our spiritual practices.

Coffee*

Coffee as a spiritual practice? Some would argue that coffee is a necessary component of all spiritual practices. Some may even consider coffee their Higher Power. Let it not be so!

This is a little whimsical, but I include coffee because of the time I spend with people over a cup of coffee. I meet with one particular friend, Sonny, for coffee on a weekly basis. As many times as we've met over the last few years, you would think Sonny and I could have solved the problems of world hunger, climate change, racism, gun violence, and peace in the Middle East … but we haven't. Instead we've shared life, provided encouragement in struggle, support in heartbreak, and guidance in decision-making. We've celebrated accomplishments, strengthened each other in faith, and laughed loud and laughed a lot. For me, coffee with Sonny and time spent with others in my home, in community coffee shops, and in local restaurants is a spiritual practice. It provides connection and strengthens us individually and in community. Try it out … you don't even have to have a seminary degree for this one! By the way, Sonny and I continued meeting for coffee online during the coronavirus pandemic because we valued this spiritual practice so much. Whatever your favorite beverage is, enjoy it with the fellowship of a friend. Get connected. Stay connected.

*Note: I must address a notation from my Chief Editor (Denise), who is not a coffee drinker. Her question was "Why not Dr. Pepper?" I think she raises a very valid point. I therefore encourage those of you "Peppers" who are reading this to take the liberty of substituting "Dr. Pepper" wherever the term Coffee is used herein. The spiritual practice of Dr. Pepper is largely supported in my household.

I hope you haven't felt "preached at." The intent of this chapter, and certainly this book, is not to evangelize, but to encourage – to encourage you to explore spirituality in whatever form it presents itself to you. As men we are conditioned to act independently. Seeking help is seen by many as an act of weakness or self-doubt. If the message hasn't been made clear by now, I've failed in my delivery. *The idea that men who need help are weak is a bold-faced lie!* If you want to win in life, you cannot do it alone. You need all the help you can get. In a world full of challenges, doesn't it make sense to use every resource at your disposal to achieve the fullness life offers? My purpose in this chapter has been to present an often overlooked resource – spirituality - which continually gives my life new direction.

Summary Points of SPIRITUALITY

- Spirituality is core to our existence.

- Spirituality and religion are not the same.

- Spirituality requires acknowledgement of a Higher Power.

- Experiencing spirituality is different for everyone.

- We are all on a spiritual journey, whether we know it or not.

- We all search for answers and a sense of connection.

- Spiritual practices can be individual or communal. Here are a
  few:
    Prayer
    Meditation
    Reading scripture and other spiritual writings
    Writing – books, poetry, songs, or journaling
    Artistic expression
    Small groups
    Worship
    Communion
    Reiki therapy
    Gratefulness
    Generosity
    Coffee

- Explore spirituality in whatever form it presents itself to you.

- Spirituality is a source of strength, not a sign of weakness.

Questions for Reflection

- How would you define your spirituality?

- What has your spiritual journey revealed to you? What has it been
  like and where do you find yourself in this journey?

- Who is someone with whom you would feel comfortable discussing spirituality? What is it about this person that makes discussion of spirituality feel safe?

- Of the spiritual practices listed in this chapter, which are you most comfortable with, if any? What is it about these practices that provides comfort?

- If you desire to expand your spiritual practices, which of these (or others) would you consider adding? Why would you find these important or worth adding?

INVITATION

Let's finish where we started. In the INTRODUCTION I pointed out how those "C'mon, man" moments can be indelibly and permanently seared into the memory. I started by talking about feeling the daily pressure not to fail. We strive for perfection in order to avoid feeling or being humiliated. Despite our efforts, there are times in all of our lives when we will feel this way. This book is not about trying to achieve perfection, it is about being better. As a matter of fact, I hope it has been a lesson in imperfection, because it wasn't written by someone who figured it all out and is now telling you how to get it right. It's written by a guy who has been transformed and is in the continuing process of being transformed, as I hope we all are. It's written by a man who wants the best for you and cares enough to be vulnerable himself if it helps you to have a higher quality of life. Because of what I've experienced and learned, I'm a better man than I was forty years ago. But I want to be a better man than I was yesterday. Better, not perfect.

You're going to get knocked down in life. It's just a matter of when. In those times there is only one thing to do – get back up and start again. Whether you're down now, getting up, or preparing for the struggle, I hope this book will help you get up, stay up, and enjoy the ride. In the INTRODUCTION I also invited you to move beyond the pressures and disappointments of the "C'mon, man" world. I want this book to be instrumental in helping you to do so. You are not meant to live a reactive or an unfulfilling life. You are meant to be the CEO of your own life.

As men we tend to live as lone wolves. We have the false impression that we should be in control of everything. We're not. We each need help. We each need support. We each need encouragement. That's what I want to do for you right now. I want you to know your essence – the core of who you are. I want you to see your potential. I want you to strive to be better every day. I want you to know you are valued and *cherished* – a word men don't often use, but should. I want you to live out of the hope and the spirit dwelling within you. I want you to recognize how loved you are and how meaningful you are to the lives of those around you. I want you to know you are powerful. I want you to know and claim control over that which is in your control. I want you to claim your life. I want you to identify and live into your purpose and meaning. I want you to see what God sees in you. Once you have done this, I want you to invite another man to do the same. I want you to be invitational. I want you to be connected to other men. In this spirit, I invite you to join me in the daily pursuit of living the life we're intended to live. C'mon, man … let's do this.

About the Author

Chris Robinson is a Licensed Professional Counselor, author and speaker from Flower Mound, Texas. He graduated from Texas A&M University in 1982 with a degree in Building Construction. After thirty-five years in the construction industry Chris felt called into the mental health profession and received his Master of Arts Degree in Professional Counseling and Marriage and Family Therapy from LeTourneau University. Chris has been married to his wife, Denise, for thirty-seven years. He has two adult daughters, Stephanie and Alyssa, and two grandchildren.

Chris is the founder and owner of Summit Counseling of North Texas, PLLC and practices in Flower Mound, Texas. He is experienced in working with children, adolescents, adults, couples, and families in the treatment of depression, anxiety, grief, relational issues, marital issues, transitions, and trauma. Primary forms of treatment include Trauma Focused Cognitive Behavioral Therapy, Cognitive Behavioral Therapy, Equine Therapy, Couples Therapy, Family Therapy, and Group Therapy. He is committed to the restoration of the relationship with self and others with the goal of restoring connections and improving quality of life by helping individuals, couples, and families work through the issues causing isolation. Chris believes spirituality is an important and beneficial element of healing and encourages clients to explore spirituality as a part of their personal journey.

For more information or to contact Chris go to
www.summitcounseling.info

Notes

Notes

Notes

Notes

Notes

Notes

Notes

Notes

Notes